MY REVISION NOTES

T-LEVELS
THE NEXT LEVEL QUALIFICATION

ENGINEERING AND MANUFACTURING

Andrew Buckenham
Andrew Topliss
David Hills-Taylor
Stephen Wilson

HODDER
Education

'T-LEVELS' is a registered trade mark of the Department for Education. 'T Level' is a registered trade mark of the Institute for Apprenticeships and Technical Education. The T Level Technical Qualification is a qualification approved and managed by the Institute for Apprenticeships and Technical Education.

The Publishers would like to thank the following for permission to reproduce copyright material.

Photo credits

Page 77 (l) © Chris Allen; **page 77 (r)** © ArtEvent ET/stock.adobe.com; **page 83** © Hrui/stock.adobe.com; **page 85 (l)** © Markus Mainka/stock.adobe.com; **page 85 (r)** © Pioneer111/stock.adobe.com; **page 101** © The British Standards Institution; **page 102** © Institute of the Motor Industry; **page 104** © Joy_Studio/Shutterstock.com; **page 120** © TheDirector/Shutterstock.com.

Although every effort has been made to ensure that website addresses are correct at time of going to press, Hodder Education cannot be held responsible for the content of any website mentioned in this book. It is sometimes possible to find a relocated web page by typing in the address of the home page for a website in the URL window of your browser.

Hachette UK's policy is to use papers that are natural, renewable and recyclable products and made from wood grown in well-managed forests and other controlled sources. The logging and manufacturing processes are expected to conform to the environmental regulations of the country of origin.

To order, please visit www.hoddereducation.com or contact Customer Service at education@hachette.co.uk / +44 (0)1235 827827.

ISBN: 978 1 3983 8519 1

First published in 2024 by
Hodder Education,
An Hachette UK Company
Carmelite House
50 Victoria Embankment
London EC4Y 0DZ

www.hoddereducation.com

Impression number   10 9 8 7 6 5 4 3 2 1

Year   2028 2027 2026 2025 2024

Cover photo © VeremeeV_1980 - stock.adobe.com

Illustrations by Integra

Typeset in India by Integra Software Services Pvt., Ltd.

Printed in Spain

A catalogue record for this title is available from the British Library.

Get the most from this book

Everyone has to decide their own revision strategy, but it is essential to review your work, learn it and test your understanding. These Revision Notes will help you do that in a planned way, topic by topic. Use this book as the cornerstone of your revision and don't hesitate to write in it – personalise your notes and check your progress by ticking off each section as you revise.

Tick to track your progress

Use the revision planner on pages 4–6 to plan your revision, topic by topic. Tick each box when you have:

+ revised and understood a topic
+ tested yourself
+ practised the exam questions and checked your answers online.

You can also keep track of your revision by ticking off each topic heading in the book. You may find it helpful to add your own notes as you work through each topic.

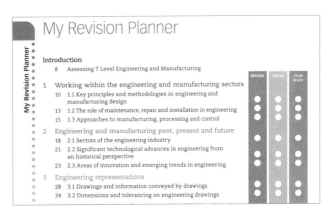

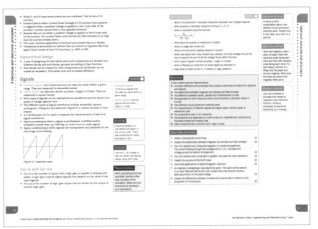

Features to help you succeed

Exam tips

Expert tips are given throughout the book to help you polish your exam technique in order to maximise your chances in the exam.

Typical mistakes

The authors identify the typical mistakes candidates make and explain how you can avoid them.

Now test yourself

These short, knowledge-based questions provide the first step in testing your learning.

Definitions and key words

Clear, concise definitions of essential key terms are provided where they first appear.

Revision activities

These activities will help you understand each topic in an interactive way.

Exam-style questions

Practice exam questions are provided for each topic. Use them to consolidate your revision and practise your exam skills.

Summaries

The summaries provide a quick-check bullet list for each topic.

Online

Go online to check your answers to the Now test yourself and Exam-style questions at **www.hoddereducation.com/myrevisionnotesdownloads**

My Revision Planner

	REVISED	TESTED	EXAM READY

1 Working within the engineering and manufacturing sectors
10 1.1 Key principles and methodologies in engineering and manufacturing design
13 1.2 The role of maintenance, repair and installation in engineering
14 1.3 Approaches to manufacturing, processing and control

2 Engineering and manufacturing past, present and future
17 2.1 Sectors of the engineering industry
20 2.2 Significant technological advances in engineering from an historical perspective
22 2.3 Areas of innovation and emerging trends in engineering

3 Engineering representations
26 3.1 Drawings and information conveyed by drawings
32 3.2 Dimensions and tolerancing on engineering drawings

4 Essential mathematics for engineering and manufacturing
35 4.1 Applied mathematical theory in engineering applications
55 4.2 Number systems used in engineering and manufacturing

5 Essential science for engineering and manufacturing
58 5.1 Units of measurement used in engineering
59 5.2 Vector and coordinate measuring systems
60 5.3 Scientific methods and approaches to scientific inquiry and research
61 5.4 Measurement equipment, techniques and principles
62 5.5 Chemical composition and behaviours
64 5.6 Forces and motion in engineering
65 5.7 Fluid dynamics in engineering
66 5.8 Thermodynamics in engineering

6 Materials and their properties
69 6.1 Physical and mechanical properties of materials
71 6.2 Types of material and their structures
74 6.3 Effects of processing techniques on materials
75 6.4 Heat treatment and surface treatments
76 6.5 Causes of material failure and their prevention
77 6.6 Materials testing methods and interpretation of results

7 Mechanical principles
79 7.1 Principles of motion and mechanics in engineering and manufacturing systems
80 7.2 Principles of forces and energy

8 Electrical and electronic principles
84 8.1 Principles of electrical and electronic systems

Check your understanding and progress at **www.hoddereducation.co.uk/myrevisionnotes**

9 Mechatronics

90 9.1 The key components of a mechatronics system

93 9.2 The operation, function and applications of programmable logic controllers in mechatronic systems

94 9.3 The basic principles of hydraulics and pneumatics

10 Engineering and manufacturing and control systems

96 10.1 Principles and applications of control system theory

99 10.2 How sensors and actuators are used in automation control systems

11 Quality management

101 11.1 Quality standards, assurance, control and improvement

108 11.2 Types and applications of standard operating procedures (SOPs) and their purposes

12 Health and safety principles and coverage

111 12.1 The main requirements of key health and safety legislation applicable to engineering activities

113 12.2 The importance of health and safety practices within the workplace

115 12.3 Responsibilities for health and safety

116 12.4 Risk assessment

118 12.5 Health and safety considerations in specific engineering contexts

121 12.6 Principles and practices relating to environmental legislation and considerations

13 Business, commercial and financial awareness

124 13.1 Principles of commercial operations and markets

125 13.2 Business and commercial practices

125 13.3 Financial and economic concepts

14 Professional responsibilities, attitudes, and behaviours

128 14.1 Professional conduct and responsibilities in the workplace

129 14.2 Continuous professional development (CPD) and professional recognition

129 14.3 Human factors within engineering and manufacturing contexts

15 Stock and asset management

132 15.1 Stock and inventory management principles and practices

133 15.2 Asset management and control principles

16 Continuous improvement

135 16.1 Continuous improvement principles and practices

REVISED   TESTED   EXAM READY

My Revision Planner

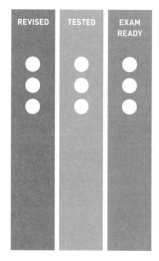

17 Project and programme management
    138 17.1 Principles of project management
    139 17.2 Roles and responsibilities in projects
    140 17.3 Project planning and control

143 Glossary

149 Index

Answers to Now test yourself and Exam-style questions online at www.hoddereducation.com/myrevisionnotesdownloads

Check your understanding and progress at **www.hoddereducation.co.uk/myrevisionnotes**

Countdown to my exams

From September

Attend class in person or via the internet if necessary; listen and enjoy the subject; make notes. Make friends in class and discuss the topics with them. Watch the news.

REVISED

6–8 weeks to go

+ Start by looking at the specification – make sure you know exactly what material you need to revise and the style of examination. Use the revision planner on pages 4–6 to familiarise yourself with the topics.
+ Organise your notes, making sure you have covered everything on the specification. The revision planner will help you to group your notes into topics.
+ Work out a realistic revision plan that will allow you time for relaxation. Set aside days and times for all the subjects that you need to study and stick to your timetable.
+ Set yourself sensible targets. Break your revision down into focused sessions of around 40 minutes, divided by breaks. These Revision Notes organise the basic facts into short, memorable sections to make revising easier.

REVISED

2–6 weeks to go

+ Read through the relevant sections of this book and refer to the exam tips, summaries, typical mistakes and key terms. Tick off the topics when you feel confident about them. Highlight those topics that you find difficult and look at them again in detail.
+ Test your understanding of each topic by working through the 'Now test yourself' questions in the book.
+ Make a note of any problem areas as you revise and ask your teacher to go over these in class.
+ Look at past papers. These provide one of the best ways to revise and practise your exam skills. Write or prepare planned answers to the Exam-style questions provided in this book.
+ Use the revision activities to try out different revision methods. For example, you can make notes using mind maps, spider diagrams or flash cards.
+ Track your progress using the revision planner and give yourself a reward when you have achieved your target.
+ Check your answers to the Now test yourself and Exam-style questions online at **www.hoddereducation.co.uk/myrevisionnotesdownloads**

REVISED

One week to go

+ Try to fit in at least one more timed practice of an entire past paper and seek feedback from your teacher, comparing your work closely with the mark scheme.
+ Check the revision planner to make sure you have not missed out any topics. Brush up on any areas of difficulty by talking them over with a friend or getting help from your teacher.
+ Attend any revision classes put on by the teacher. Remember, they are an expert at preparing people for examinations.

REVISED

The day before the examination

+ Flick through these Revision Notes for useful reminders, for example, the exam tips, summaries, typical mistakes and key terms.
+ IMPORTANT: Check the time (is it in the morning or afternoon?) and place of your examination. Keep in touch with other students in your class.
+ Make sure you have everything you need for the exam – pens, highlighters and water.
+ Allow some time to relax and have an early night to ensure you are fresh and alert.

REVISED

My exams

Paper 1
Date:..
Time: ....
Location: ....

Paper 2
Date:..
Time: ....
Location: ....

Introduction

Assessing T Level Engineering and Manufacturing

This book supports the assessment of the Core Component of the following qualifications:

✚ T Level Technical Qualification in Maintenance, Installation and Repair for Engineering and Manufacturing (8712)
✚ T Level Technical Qualification in Engineering, Manufacturing, Processing and Control (8713)
✚ T Level Technical Qualification in Design and Development for Engineering and Manufacturing (8714)

The assessment of the Core Component comprises:

✚ Paper 1 (35% core grade)
✚ Paper 2 (35% core grade)

Both exams include a range of short-answer and extended-response questions.

In addition to these papers there is an employer-set project worth 90 marks that contributes 30% to the overall Core Component grade. The employer-set project consists of a real industry-style brief that will require the use of relevant maths, English and digital skills. It will enable the learner to demonstrate their knowledge and understanding of the core content and their core skills to solve occupationally relevant situations and/or problems.

In the second year, there is also an occupational specialist component. This synoptic assignment consists of a project brief presented as client requirements or a specification of work to enable the learner to demonstrate the full range of their knowledge and relevant skills. The Occupational Specialism assessment is set and marked against several assessment themes that contribute towards the final mark.

Command words

REVISED ○

Familiarity with the relevant command words is important and helps the learner to avoid wasting time in the exam room, for example by trying to evaluate when there is no requirement for it. The most frequently used command words for the T Level papers are:

✚ **Identify, State:** These require just one or two words or a short phrase, and typically there is just 1 mark per point required. For example: Identify two variables. [2 marks]
✚ **Describe:** This requires a more detailed, descriptive response and is typically worth 2 marks.
✚ **Justify:** This is often used together with Identify and requires you to justify the answer you have given. For example: Identify a constant and justify why it is declared as a constant. [3 marks]
✚ **Explain:** This is asking for more than a description and requires you include the connections or relationships between relevant factors. It may be worth 2, 3 or more marks. You should provide the same number of different, relevant points in your response as the number of marks available. For example: Explain a benefit of pattern recognition. [3 marks] You could, for example, describe one benefit, then go on to explain why it is a benefit.

- **Compare:** This is asking you to describe or explain the similarities and differences between two items.
- **Discuss, Evaluate, Analyse:** These indicate a long answer is required and are typically worth 6 or more marks. These questions will not be marked simply on the statement of facts but on the depth of the discussion in the response. It is important that all aspects of the question are answered in some detail and it is a good idea to identify the component parts of the question before starting a response.

Additional guidance

If asked to **give examples**, make sure they are relevant to the scenario.

When asked to provide program code or diagrams, always plan your approach first.

This exam includes many technical topics, and you should always use the correct **technical terminology**.

Always read the question carefully before starting a response. The key words used in the questions will provide some clues to what the examiner is expecting from the answer.

The T Level exam papers

The two exams covered by this book are each 2 hours and 30 minutes long and each is worth 100 marks. Each externally set paper contributes 35% of the overall core grade.

Paper 1
- Unit 4 Essential mathematics for engineering and manufacturing
- Unit 5 Essential science for engineering and manufacturing
- Unit 6 Materials and their properties
- Unit 7 Mechanical principles
- Unit 8 Electrical and electronic principles
- Unit 9 Mechatronics

Paper 2
- Unit 1 Working within the engineering and manufacturing sectors
- Unit 2 Engineering and manufacturing past, present and future
- Unit 3 Engineering representations
- Unit 10 Engineering and manufacturing and control systems
- Unit 11 Quality management
- Unit 12 Health and safety principles and coverage
- Unit 13 Business, commercial and financial awareness
- Unit 14 Professional responsibilities, attitudes, and behaviours
- Unit 15 Stock and asset management
- Unit 16 Continuous improvement
- Unit 17 Project and programme management

1 Working within the engineering and manufacturing sectors

1.1 Key principles and methodologies in engineering and manufacturing design

Types of manufacturing processes

Table 1.1 Types of manufacturing processes

Type of manufacturing process	Explanation of terminology
Wasting	A term for a process which involves the removal of unnecessary sections of material from a product to make way for a new component, for example drilling or sawing of steel bar.
Forming	The bending, twisting and beating of material that forces the shape of the material to change. Examples of forming are found in sheet-steel manufacturing techniques.
Shaping	Casting and moulding processes
Joining	The joining of two or more components to make a larger assembly with e.g., bolts, screws and nuts. Other methods for joining include adhesives and welds.
Finishing	The quality of the surface finish. Can be checked with tactile gauges. A better surface finish will take more time to machine. Linishing, emery cloth and polishing are tools and techniques which can be used to improve surface finish.
Casting	The use of moulds and molten metal to produce complex shapes.
Additive manufacturing	3D printing of plastic, metal and even concrete. Layers are created and then built up into solid 3D shapes.

The design process

The design process involves research, development, testing and a little inspiration.

User requirements

Does the final design do what is needed? Is it robust enough? Does it meet legislation and standards? Does it meet the budget? Does it meet environmental requirements? Can your company manufacture it? Does it meet the specification? Does the customer like it?

Design brief

This is a document from the customer, or created by you with the customer, which gives a short (brief) statement of what is being designed. It is usually light on detail but will contain some requirements and constraints for the final product.

Specification

The specification follows after the design brief, and also after research and development has taken place. The specification sets out the goals of the project so that at the end the resulting product can be measured against it. It is specific in its presentation of measurements. For example, the specification does not state that the final product 'will be small' but states that 'it will be a minimum size of 100 × 200 × 50 mm and a maximum of 200 × 300 × 100 mm'.

Check your understanding and progress at **www.hoddereducation.co.uk/myrevisionnotes**

Approaches to design

Table 1.2 Design methodologies

Design methodology	Explanation of terminology
Linear design (see Figure 1.1)	A step-by-step design solution, e.g. 1) client brief, 2) product design specification (PDS), 3) investigation, 4) idea generation, 5) development of product, 6) manufacture of product, 7) product testing stage, 8) evaluation of process.
Iterative design (see Figure 1.2)	A cyclic process where products are designed, made and evaluated, which feeds back into the design. For example, after creating the specification, testing shows that one of the goals is not possible. This result prompts the move to revise the specification and start the process again.
Design for manufacturing and assembly (DFMA)	This design method aims to provide good design at a lower cost. There are five areas which are looked at in the DFMA process: 1) process, 2) design, 3) material, 4) environment, 5) compliance/testing.

By including everyone involved in the process: engineers, machine operators, suppliers, tooling makers, etc., the design can be examined at all levels to avoid the possibility of repeating existing mistakes or defects. Making changes earlier in the design process will have a bigger impact and cost less. |
Ergonomic design	This type of product design accounts for human safety and comfort.
Anthropometric data	The designing of products where importance is given to the measurement of different parts of the human body. It is a term derived from Greek: *anthro-* people, *metric-* measurement.
Inclusive design	The design process that attempts to create products that are available for the widest audience possible (including people with physical and mental disabilities).
Sustainable design	This type of design concentrates on producing products in an environmentally considerate fashion, minimising use of energy and natural materials. The sustainable designer must keep in mind the '6Rs': reduce (production of waste and energy use), refuse (to use harmful materials or processes), rethink (the approach used in designing the product), repair (design products that can be repaired and have their life extended), reuse (avoid designing single-use products that need to be disposed of) and recycle (have the ability to break down the product when it reaches the end of its life and recycle the waste).

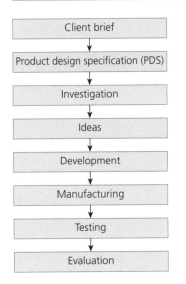

Figure 1.1 The linear design process

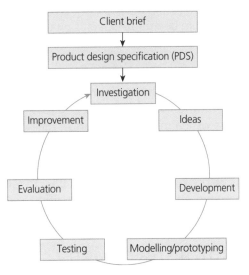

Figure 1.2 The iterative design cycle

Revision activity

Have a careful look at an item on your desk. Is it fit for purpose? Does it function correctly? Is it aesthetically pleasing (does it look good)? Is it durable? What could be improved? It is good practice to think about the function of products: why they are a particular shape, why they are made from a particular material, what their manufacturing process is and how it could be improved.

Iterative To take the output from a process, evaluate the results and use this information to improve the process/design.

Anthropometric data Values relating to people across a wide range of sizes and abilities, for example the height and reach of the population.

Sustainable A process which can be carried out for a long period of time, usually in an environmentally friendly context. For example, in a sustainable forest, trees are planted to replace those that are chopped down.

Typical mistake

A product should always be designed so that it can be used by most of the population, that is the 5th percentile to the 95th percentile, **not** the average person (50th percentile), which is just the middle of the distribution curve (see Figure 1.3). Figure 1.4 is a diagram showing anthropometric data. Tables are available showing measurements for different percentiles.

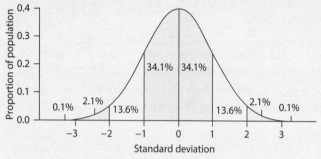

Figure 1.3 A standard normal distribution curve

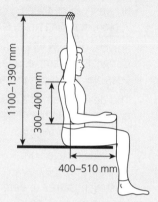

Figure 1.4 A person showing some sample dimensions

Research and testing methodologies

REVISED

Primary sources

Primary research is what you find out first hand, from questions asked in surveys to results from product tests.

Secondary sources

These are results obtained by others. For example, standard data about material strength from a reliable source is secondary data.

Both of these types of research data can be quantitative or qualitative.

Testing

When designing a new test, the following should be considered: what is the end point? What is the information which the test needs to show? (For example, this test will show the condition of the product after five years of use). Is the test fair? Are all factors which might help achieve the desired result taken into account? Is the test accurate? How much confidence can you place in the results?

Thinking about these questions before research begins will help to retain focus on what needs to be researched, the time needed for testing and the cost implications.

Methods of communicating design requirements

REVISED

The audience for the product must always be considered. Who will be looking at the information? A technical specification would be appropriate for a design engineer, but a summary might be needed for the director or the marketing team. Detail drawings are required for manufacture but not to communicate the product to the customer.

> **Quantitative data** Research about things which can be measured in numbers. How fast, tall, heavy, expensive?
>
> **Qualitative data** Research about things which can be described. What do users think? Does the product look attractive? Is it easy to use?

> **Detail drawing** A detail drawing shows all the information needed for manufacture.

Check your understanding and progress at **www.hoddereducation.co.uk/myrevisionnotes**

1.2 The role of maintenance, repair and installation in engineering

Types of maintenance

REVISED ●

Table 1.3 Types of maintenance

Type of Maintenance	Description
Planned or preventative	Both planned and **preventative maintenance** are carried out to a predetermined schedule. This could be time based, e.g. the machine will be serviced every six months, or could be based on usage, e.g. a car will be serviced every 10000 km. Preventative maintenance will make greater use of data gathered from inspection of parts and monitoring of the machine to help schedule when maintenance needs to take place.
Reactive	This type of maintenance is undertaken at the point of machine failure – the fix is a reaction to the situation. Reactive maintenance requires a contingency plan. Spare parts can be purchased in advance (e.g. drill bits) and stored away for emergency use. For small consumables this is a valid maintenance technique. For example, if a drill bit breaks, this can replaced quickly and easily. A disadvantage of reactive maintenance is that the machine will have to be stopped for it to be carried out and thus production time will be lost.
Condition-based monitoring	This concentrates on real-time monitoring and analysis of large amounts of data to determine when maintenance needs to take place. The focus of the monitoring is on the tolerance levels of the machine. This could include noise, vibration and heat monitoring. When a change in these levels is identified, then maintenance is scheduled. This will often be coupled with software analysis.

Now test yourself TESTED ●

1 Explain the advantages and disadvantages of reactive maintenance.
2 What is a disadvantage of condition-based maintenance?
3 What kinds of process would reactive maintenance be appropriate for?
4 What are the 'six Rs' and how can they be applied?
5 Why are the six Rs and other tools and legislation aimed at sustainability increasingly important?
6 What is the iterative design process?

> **Maintenance** To keep something in good working order and repair.
>
> **Preventative** To stop problems which might happen if nothing was done.

Roles and functions

REVISED ●

Table 1.4 Roles and functions

Role	Responsibility
Machine operator	Responsible for day-to-day operation of machinery. This includes daily maintenance (e.g. lubrication, monitoring of levels). The machine operator is responsible for reporting any immediate concerns about the functioning of the equipment or safety to the maintenance manager.
Maintenance engineer/ manager	Engineers plan and schedule when maintenance should happen in order to minimise disruption. They may also repair and maintain the equipment in a scheduled fashion. Systems will be completely shut down in order for the engineers to carry out their job.

Tools, equipment and measuring

Table 1.5 Tools and equipment

Type of tool	Example
Portable power tools	Drill, angle grinder, soldering iron
Hand tools	Spanner, screwdriver, pliers, wire cutters, hammers
Measuring instruments and gauges	Tape measures, infrared thermometers, flow meters, multimeters, steel rules

Installation and commissioning

Traditionally in engineering and construction, commissioning is the process of ensuring that the finished system is fit for purpose and can be handed over to the customer. It involves trials, tests, checks and inspection that guarantee the safe and smooth running of the machinery. Once the completed product has been installed and signed off, the client becomes responsible for the safe running and maintenance of the machine.

1.3 Approaches to manufacturing, processing and control

Scale of manufacture

Table 1.6 Differing scales of manufacturing

Differing scales of manufacture	Batch size
One-off	As the name suggests, only one or two items are made. The product will often demand highly skilled manual workmanship and command a high price tag. The item might also be a prototype for a product in development.
Batch	Small volume manufacture. Typically, there is some automation of process but skilled manual work will be required as well. Batch production can also be small volume and therefore high cost, e.g. Morgan cars or personalised T-shirts.
Mass production	A high-volume, largely automated production system which produces products of the same quality. Dedicated machines are necessary for each process, for example mass car production.
Continuous production	The material never stops being manufactured. Compared with mass production where the product may stop at a station to have work done to it, in continuous production there is no stopping. The system will usually be designed to produce just one product. Often used in chemical manufacture or food manufacture, e.g. spaghetti.

> **Revision activity**
>
> For the following products, find out how they are manufactured and which method of production fits them best:
> + toothpaste
> + Morgan cars
> + light bulbs.

Manufacturing infrastructure

Table 1.7 Type and purpose of manufacturing layout

Type of manufacturing layout	Purpose of layout (advantages and limitations)
Matrix production system	A combination of functional and cellular systems. Machines of the same type may be grouped together, with some other machines needed to add features to specific products next to them.
Cellular manufacturing	This is where all the different machines and processes needed to make a product are grouped together, minimising the distance that products travel within the factory.
Functional	This is where machines of the same type are grouped together to capitalise on the skill of the operators.
Product/production line	A high-volume equivalent of a manufacturing cell, that just manufactures a single type of product.

Levels of automation

REVISED

Table 1.8 Different levels of automation

Type of automation	Description
Computer aided manufacture (CAM)	Often used with computer aided design (CAD), CAD/CAM allows the design and testing process to be accelerated, as testing and simulation can be done on a computer without the need to manufacture. CAM encompasses the use of computer numerically controlled (CNC) machining as well as robotic systems. CAM allows a greater precision and higher volume than traditional methods but will have a higher cost to put systems in place.
Manual system	Does not use automation at all. A manual system can be very flexible in its approach, although these systems are expensive because of the need to use highly skilled workers.
Fully automated	Used in the continuous manufacturing process, a system is created to manufacture a single product. This type of manufacture produces large volumes and is never turned off.
Robotic	A system that uses a flexible, fast 'arm' to run a series of repeated movements and produce large amounts of the product. The robot can be reprogrammed to work on different products and carry out tasks quickly, for example placing items in boxes, riveting components or spot welding.

1 Working within the engineering and manufacturing sectors

15

Table 1.9 Control measures

Type of control measure	Description
Performance monitoring	A proactive data collection method that forms the basis of statistical process control (SPC). SPC looks at trends and identifies problems in the system or on the build line. The goal is to identify problems early on and correct any possible issues that crop up.
Quality control (QC)	Checks made during the process of manufacture. These checks include compliance with the **specification**, goods-inward inspections (where components for the final product are received and checked for fitness), in-process inspections (checks for manufacturing errors) and finished goods inspections (so that the product is signed off before arriving with the purchaser).
Quality assurance (QA)	These checks include performance monitoring, overseeing QC checks, identification of the main causes of quality issues and the planning of elimination of these issues (by redesigning processes).

Summary

In this content area you learned about:

✚ the design process, from the initial conversation with the customer and the writing of the design brief to the creation of a specification, development, iteration and the consideration which goes into the final solution for a finished product

✚ how engineering manufacturing processes can be maintained, what techniques are used to reduce the time that machines are switched off for maintenance and servicing. What is measured and why?

✚ how products are manufactured, the different ways factories can be laid out and how parts move through a factory, what processes are undertaken and in what order.

Specification A document that states how the component must perform, e.g. maximum size, material, cost.

Exam-style questions

1 List and define the six Rs in sustainable design and explain their importance in the manufacturing industry. [3]

2 Explain the role of the design brief when designing a product. [2]

3 What are the advantages of sustainable design? [3–4]

4 Describe the different types of manufacturing layout. [2]

5 What are the advantages to testing using software? [2]

6 What types of manufacturing, automation and control would be suitable for manufacturing a ballpoint pen? [1]

   Why are these methods more suitable than other alternatives? [3]

7 What does sustainable design mean? Why is it becoming more important and what might the impacts of this be? [4]

2 Engineering and manufacturing past, present and future

2.1 Sectors of the engineering industry

The engineering profession covers a wide range of industrial sectors, including manufacturing metal products, manufacturing machinery and equipment, electronics, electrical equipment, transportation equipment and instruments.

Table 2.1 gives examples of key engineering sectors.

Table 2.1 Key engineering sectors

Engineering sector	Main activities of the engineer	Products and/or services
Automotive	Research and development, design, manufacture and maintenance	Cars, motorbikes, trucks and other road-going vehicles
Aerospace	Responsible for the design and structure of air transport vehicles, such as aeroplanes, spacecraft or satellites	Civil aircraft Military aircraft Helicopters Uncrewed aerial vehicles (UAVs) Missiles Spacecraft
Agriculture	Build, service and repair agricultural, horticultural and forestry machinery and equipment. Design climate and irrigation systems to maximise crop yields.	Agricultural machinery and equipment Supervision of building projects, e.g. land drainage, reclamation and irrigation Designing vehicles for all ground and weather conditions Test and install new equipment, e.g. harvester and crop sprayers
Chemical	Develop and experiment with machines and plants, which lead to chemical reactions in order to create valuable products and solve everyday problems	Petrol and diesel Antibiotics and vaccines Plastics Fertiliser Drinking water
Control	Analyse and design complex control systems that include mechanical, electrical, chemical, metallurgical, electronic, and pneumatic components	Robotics Control systems in transport, e.g. aircraft Manufacturing assembly lines
Defence	Responsible for the design and production of military equipment, vehicles and systems	Tanks Missile systems Guns Vehicles
Electrical	Focus on the design and manufacture of electrical systems for buildings, transport and construction	Electrical system design, e.g. an assembly line control system, manufacture and implementation

Engineering sector	Main activities of the engineer	Products and/or services
Electronic	Deal with the circuitry and tiny intricacies of electronics	Mobile phones Portable music devices Computers Robotics Electrical equipment
Logistics	Dedicated to the scientific organisation of the purchase, transport, storage, distribution, and warehousing of materials and finished goods	Transportation from manufacturer to warehouse Storage and warehousing Order fulfilment Shipping to customers
Manufacturing	Turn raw materials into new products. Research and develop new manufacturing processes, machines, tools and equipment	Used by many industries such as: Food and drink **Pharmaceuticals** Oil
Marine	Design and production of ships, boats, oilrigs and other offshore vessels	Ships Boats Oilrigs and other offshore installations Main propulsion engines
Materials	Carry out research, specification development and design of materials which allow various technologies to progress	Engineering materials Metal alloys Plastics Ceramics
Medical	Check medical equipment to make sure it is working properly and is safe to use	Acceptance testing of new equipment Introducing equipment and devices into service Advising on the correct use of equipment Addressing patient safety issues Safely disposing of old devices
Petrochemical	Involved with the production of hydrocarbons such as natural gas or crude oil, petroleum, oil and gas	Natural gas Crude oil Petroleum Oil and gas
Power generation from non-renewables	Responsible for the generation of electricity using non-renewable energy sources	Power from non-renewable energy sources includes: Petroleum Natural gas Coal **Hydrocarbon gas liquids**
Power generation from renewables	Responsible for the generation of electricity using renewable energy sources	Power from renewable energy sources: Solar energy from the Sun Geothermal energy from inside the Earth Wind energy **Biomass** from plants Hydropower from flowing water

Check your understanding and progress at **www.hoddereducation.co.uk/myrevisionnotes**

Engineering sector	Main activities of the engineer	Products and/or services
Power generation from nuclear sources	Responsible for the safety and efficiency of nuclear power plants	Power from nuclear energy sources, e.g. electrical generation from a power station
Rail	Responsible for the maintenance and improvement of railway systems around the country	Signalling systems Track building and maintenance Overhead line systems Rolling stock maintenance
Structural	Deal with the construction, design and maintenance of load-bearing structures	Public buildings Bridges Housing
Telecommunications	Design and develop communication networks for voice, data and multimedia applications	Satellite systems Digital TV and **fibre optics** systems Broadband and mobile installation Landline phone networks
Water management	Design and supervise the construction of water supply and water treatment/sewage systems	Sewerage plant maintenance Water treatment Flood defence structures Pump and pipework systems
Waste management	Provide a service for all engineering waste including metal (**ferrous** and **non-ferrous**), oils, greases, contaminated rags and solvents	Safe disposal of toxic material Disposal of metal Disposal of contaminated rags and solvents

Metallurgical Relating to the scientific study of the structures and uses of metals.

Pneumatic Operated by air or gas under pressure.

Pharmaceuticals Compounds manufactured for use as medicinal drugs.

Hydrocarbon gas liquids Liquids made from natural gas and crude oil.

Biomass Combustible renewable energy sources including plants, organic materials and animal waste.

Fibre optics Technology that transmits information as light pulses along a glass or plastic fibre.

Ferrous Metals that contain iron, e.g. steel.

Non-ferrous Metals that contain no iron, e.g. copper.

> **Typical mistake**
>
> Make sure you do not confuse renewable energy sources with non-renewable energy sources. Renewables are derived from natural resources that are replenished while non-renewable energy sources will run out.

> **Exam tip**
>
> You will need to give an overview of the main activities provided by each engineering sector, for example know the typical products and services supplied.

> **Now test yourself**   TESTED ○
>
> 1 Which engineering sector makes motorbikes?
> 2 State one non-renewable energy resource.
> 3 Which engineering sector develops robotics?
> 4 Give one example of biomass.
> 5 Which engineering sector designs sewerage plants?

> **Revision activity**
>
> Research the medical sector to identify what new technologies are being developed to improve medical care, for example, remote surgery and the 3D printing of skin and organs.

2.2 Significant technological advances in engineering from an historical perspective

Engineers have benefitted from technological advances throughout history, and this has contributed to social and economic development. Innovative developments have been made in a number of areas. For example, engineering materials such as composites have developed over the years allowing an increasing range of new products to be manufactured (see Figure 2.1).

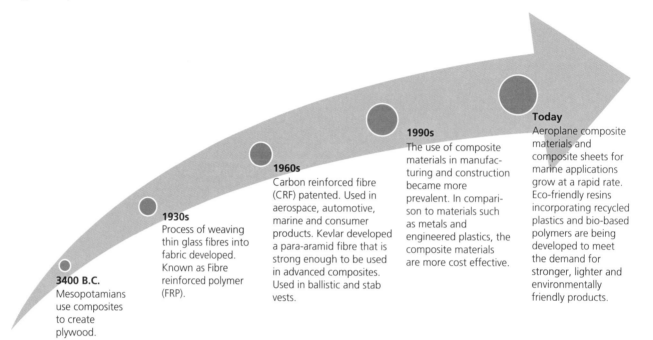

Figure 2.1 History of composites

Table 2.2 Key advances in technology

Technology	Key advances
Electrical power	Industrial revolution in the 18th century powered by coal and steam.
	Hydro-electric power and solar power developed in the 19th century.
	In the 20th century, the UK mainly generated electrical power by burning coal.
	In 2019, in both the UK and the USA, more energy was generated from zero-carbon sources than from fossil fuels.
Electrical sources of artificial lighting	The first electric incandescent bulb was commercially developed in the 19th century.
	In 1934, **fluorescent lighting** was developed.
	In the 1960s, **light-emitting diodes (LEDs)** were developed.
	LEDs require less energy to produce light with lower energy bills and less impact on the environment.
Electric motors	The first official battery-powered electric motor was invented in 1834.
	In 1886, the first practical DC motor that could run at constant speed under variable loads was produced.
	In 1892, the first practical **induction motor** was designed, making the unit suitable for use in automotive applications.
	In the 21st century, electric motors are now widely used in industries across the globe and are an integral part of many applications, from powered wheelchairs and stairlifts to industrial automation and transport.

Check your understanding and progress at **www.hoddereducation.co.uk/myrevisionnotes**

Technology	Key advances
The internal combustion engine	The gas vacuum engine was the first internal combustion engine, designed in 1823.
	Commercial drilling and petroleum production started in the 1850s.
	In 1886, the commercially produced petrol-operated engines for vehicles which used internal combustion were installed.
	These inventions enabled the development of the car, train, ship, and aeroplane, allowing mass mobility to flourish. Transportation paved the way for a steadily rising global exchange of goods and people.
Replaceable parts and mass production	In 1798, Eli Whitney built a firearms factory in the USA. His workmen made the first muskets with the standardised, interchangeable parts of modern mass production methods.
	The invention of interchangeable parts contributed to the Industrial Revolution.
	Parts were made by machine to be exactly the same size and shape. Any part could fit into any product of the same design. This led to mass production where products could be made easier, cheaper and faster.
Development of materials	Industry demands have driven the development of materials. Mechanical performance improvements and cost reductions are two of the most important factors. Key material developments over the years have included composites, nanomaterials and polymers. + Composites: see figure 2.1 for key developments. + Nanomaterials: in 1830, Michael Faraday invented colloidal gold, a liquid containing tiny gold particles (what we now call nanoparticles). Fullerenes were discovered in 1985 and are an important structure in nanomaterials. Cylinders of fullerenes, only a few nanometres wide, allowed carbon nanotubes to be discovered in 1991. In 2002, carbon nanotubes were used to replace metal wires on microchips for the first time.
Television (TV)	In the 1920s, the first public demonstration of televised silhouette images in motion was given from mechanical televisions that used a rotating disc with holes.
	The electronic TV captured images in 1927 using a beam of electrons, basically a simple camera. This technology was called a cathode ray tube (CRT) and valves were used to control the flow of the electric current.
	All images on a TV were black and white until colour televisions became commercially available in the UK in 1969.
	TVs began to use light-emitting diode (LED) technology in the early 1990s when blue LED lights were invented.
	Organic light-emitting diode (OLED) TVs became popular in the early 2000s and have greatly improved image quality, higher brightness and an ultra-thin display; they also have lower power consumption.
	4K and 5K displays allow ultra-high definition (UHD) that can be displayed on very large TV screens.
Radio	The first practical radio transmitters and receivers were developed around 1895, though limited to coded dots and dashes, and used for Morse code.
	In 1906, the first long-distance transmission of human voice and music took place.
	Since the 1980s, the electrics have transformed into electronic circuits creating Digital Audio Broadcasting (DAB).
Automated machines	The automation of machines had its beginnings in the Industrial Revolution and describes the reduction of human intervention in processes.
	In 1771, Richard Arkwright invented the first fully automated spinning mill driven by water power.
	Conveyor belts have been used since the late 19th century to move coal, ore and other raw materials.
	In the 20th century, industrial robots and robotic arms have been introduced to allow automated manual handling (AMH).

Technology	Key advances
Computers and the internet	The internet was created in 1983 and prior to this time, the various computer networks did not have a standard way to communicate with each other.
	The internet was first invented for military purposes and then expanded to the purpose of communication among scientists. The invention also came about, in part, due to the increasing need for computers in the 1960s.
	The internet helps with facts and figures, information and knowledge for personal, social and economic development.

Hydro-electric power A renewable source of energy that generates power using a dam to alter the natural flow of a river or other body of water.

Fluorescent lighting A low-pressure mercury-vapour gas-discharge lamp that uses fluorescence to produce visible light.

Light-emitting diodes (LEDs) A semiconductor device that emits light when current flows through it.

Induction motor An alternating-current motor.

Synthetic An artificial substance or material.

> **Exam tip**
>
> Make sure you remember at least three key advances for each technology, for example transportation, healthcare and housing.

> **Typical mistake**
>
> Questions will often ask you to give the full name of acronyms. Make sure you know all required acronyms, such as AMH, meaning automated manual handling.

Now test yourself TESTED ○

6 What does the acronym LED stand for?
7 What does O stand for in the acronym OLED?

2.3 Areas of innovation and emerging trends in engineering

Innovation and emerging trends are evolving and could influence manufacturing, environmental considerations, social and economic development. Technological advancements can help engineers carry out their jobs more efficiently and facilitate innovation.

> **Chatbots (or chatterbot)** A software application used to conduct an online chat conversation via text or text-to-speech.

Table 2.3 Areas of innovation and emerging trends

Areas of innovation	Emerging trends
Artificial intelligence (AI)	Self-driving cars
Computer systems with AI can perform tasks that would normally require human intelligence, including visual perception, speech recognition, decision-making and language translation.	Online shopping
	Healthcare technology
	Chatbots
	Streaming services
	Factory and warehousing systems
	Educational tools

Areas of innovation	Emerging trends
Virtual reality (VR) VR allows users to experience 3D environments virtually while interacting with them, so that they seem to be immersed in them at all times.	Automotive design
	Healthcare
	Shopping online
	Tourism
	Interior design
	Gambling
	Training and education
	Entertainment
Augmented reality (AR) AR is an immersive digital experience of the physical world that combines digital visual, audio or other **sensory stimuli**.	Retail to promote products and services
	Education
	Navigation
	Manufacturing sector, e.g. stock control, expert support, maintenance
	Hands-free operation of a smartphone, e.g. access the internet, record a video or take a photo
Digitalisation Digitalisation is the conversion of text, pictures or sound into a digital form that can be processed by a computer and then used to improve business processes.	Enabling the automation of machines
	Scanning paper documents to allow access to a greater audience
	Improving quality control testing through faster data collection
Robotics The design, construction, and use of machines (robots) to perform tasks. A high proportion of these tasks do not replicate human actions. In many cases robots are used to do things humans cannot do.	Manufacturing
	Mining
	Automotive
	Aerospace
	Healthcare
	Warehousing
Autonomous systems Autonomous systems are self-controlling (automatic) and not reliant on any direct human intervention.	AI systems and drones are autonomous as they can make individual decisions based on their embedded computer systems and sensor array
Drones Drones are flying robots that can be remotely controlled or fly autonomously using software-controlled flight plans in their embedded computer systems. Uncrewed Aerial Systems (UAVs) are most often associated with the armed forces and can only operate with human intervention.	Surveillance and intelligence gathering
	Shopping deliveries
	Agriculture
	Emergency rescue
	Photography
Distributed energy Distributed energy refers to small generation units that are near to where they will be used, i.e. a home or business.	Roof top solar **photovoltaic (PV)** units
	Wind-powered generating units
	Emergency backup generators, usually powered by petrol/diesel fuel
	Battery storage
Hybrid technologies Hybrid technology systems combine two or more technologies with the aim of achieving more efficient systems.	Wind–solar photovoltaic (PV) hybrid systems
	Wind–diesel hybrid systems
	Fuel-cell–gas-turbine hybrid systems
	Wind–fuel-cell hybrid systems
	Petrol and electricity hybrid car systems

Areas of innovation	Emerging trends
Cyber-physical systems (CPS) Cyber-physical systems allow physical objects to connect to the internet and each other using sensors, control and networking.	Robots Intelligent buildings Implantable medical devices Cars that drive themselves Planes that automatically fly in a controlled airspace
The internet of things (IOT) IOT describes the network of physical objects (things) that are embedded with sensors, software and other technologies for the purpose of connecting to and exchanging data with other devices and systems over the internet.	Connected appliances in the home Autonomous farming equipment Wearable health monitors Wireless stock trackers Smart factory equipment **Biometric** cybersecurity scanners Ultra-high-speed wireless internet
Cloud computing Cloud computing is the use of a network of remote servers to store, manage, and process data, rather than independent personal computers.	Allows the access of applications and data from any location worldwide and from any device.
Sustainability Sustainability is the development of a product while trying to reduce negative impacts on the environment. Engineers look at how a product might affect the environment through its life cycle and try to work with the 6 Rs of sustainability.	6 Rs of sustainability: Reduce Reuse Recycle Rethink Refuse Repair
Product life cycle This encompasses the various stages of a product's evolution, from its beginning to its end.	Raw-material extraction Manufacturing Use End-of-life recycling
Circular economy The circular economy is a system to reduce the impact of the use of materials on the environment. It reduces waste and pollution by reusing and recycling materials.	Design Manufacture User Recycle
Exploring alternatives New technologies continue to be developed and alternative solutions for many problems are being researched and developed.	Use of sustainable plastics for bottles and packaging Use of sustainable concrete in buildings Use of sustainable glass from oranges
Renewables Renewables are a natural resource or source of energy that is not depleted by use, such as water, wind, or solar power.	Biomass energy Hydropower Geothermal power
Waste and disposal Waste disposal has challenged engineers for many years as it is a major contributor to climate change. The main methods of waste disposal are landfill, reuse and recycling.	Generating power from waste is one of the major innovations in the waste-management industry. This technique aims to convert waste into energy instead of adding to the growing amount of waste in landfill sites. Using AI-enabled robots to sort through recyclable waste minimises the health risks to humans.

Check your understanding and progress at **www.hoddereducation.co.uk/myrevisionnotes**

Sensory stimuli Any event or object that is received by the senses and elicits a response from a person.

Photovoltaic (PV) The conversion of light into electricity using semiconducting materials.

Biometric Body measurements and calculations related to human characteristics.

Now test yourself

TESTED

8 What are hybrid technologies?

9 What does the acronym AI stand for?

10 What term describes machines that replicate human actions?

11 What does the acronym VR stand for?

Summary

In this content area you learned about:

+ sectors of the engineering industry
+ significant technological advances in engineering from a historical perspective
+ areas of innovation and emerging trends in engineering.

Exam-style questions

1   State **one** product produced by the chemical engineering sector. [1]

2   Name the engineering sector that produces hydrocarbon fuels. [1]

3   Describe what is meant by the term 'autonomous systems'. [1]

4   Name the types of molecules found in polymers. [1]

5   Drones use GPS. State what the acronym GPS stands for. [1]

6   Describe what biomass consists of. [2]

7   State the term given to the conversion of text or sound to be processed by a computer. [1]

8   Describe what is meant by the term 'distributed energy'. [2]

9   Define what is meant by the product life cycle. [1]

10 State what the acronym AR stands for. [1]

11 Explain **two** ways in which the circular economy tackles climate change. [2]

12 Give **two** examples of practical applications of the internet of things. [2]

13 Explain **three** benefits of cloud computing for social and economic development. [4]

14 Discuss how the development of virtual reality may influence engineering activities in the future. [8]

Typical mistake

Ensure you fully understand that **sustainability** is not just about waste and disposal but also refers to product life cycle, exploring alternatives, renewables and the circular economy.

Exam tip

Questions may ask about areas of innovation within engineering. Make sure you focus on two to three key emerging trends for the area of innovation stated in the question.

Revision activity

Carry out online research to find out what the product life cycle is for a smartphone. What materials can be recycled and what materials are unusable?

---

3 Engineering representations

3.1 Drawings and information conveyed by drawings

Types of engineering drawing

An engineering drawing is typically created in orthographic projection and is either a detail drawing or an assembly drawing. Pictorial drawing techniques can also be used to communicate ideas, for example an isometric drawing.

> **Exam tip**
>
> BS: British Standards are produced by the British Standards Institute. The standards cover everything from cricket balls to engineering drawing. Other common standards are EN: European Normal; ISO: International Standards Organisation; ANSI: American National Standards Institute. Some standards are used by more than one standards body.

> **Orthographic** This refers to the style of drawing used by engineers to communicate complex designs. Two-dimensional views of the different surfaces are laid out in line with each other.

Table 3.1 Types of engineering drawings

Type of drawing	Description
Detail drawing	A representation of a three-dimensional object presented in a number of two-dimensional (orthographic) drawing views, including all the information needed to manufacture. Orthographic drawings give multiple views of a design (e.g. front of the part, left of the part, top of the part, etc.) as this allows all necessary information to be easily communicated.
Freehand drawing	Hand-drawn representations, usually used to quickly show ideas and iterate them.
Assembly drawing	This type of engineering drawing shows how everything fits together (see Figure 3.2). It may use section views, bills of materials (BOMs) and numbered arrows to list and highlight all the parts and quantities needed for the finished product.
Isometric	Isometric drawing is used to present three-dimensional objects. There are no horizontal lines; the depth lines go back at 30°. It is useful for communicating a design in a way which can be understood by most people.
Computer aided design (CAD)	A type of software used to make 3D designs that are visible from any angle. Advantages over hand-drawing techniques for engineering drawing are the level of accuracy and the ease with which a part of the design can be altered.
Exploded views	A set of isometric drawings that have an explosive appearance. The drawings show components of a product and illustrate how the components are assembled.
Block diagrams	These diagrams give a high-level overview of the relationships between parts, systems or functions. Visually, they do not have the appearance of a product or its parts.
Flowcharts	A flowchart can be used to plot a decision process or help work out the steps needed to get to an answer.
Circuit diagrams	Circuit diagrams show the layout, connections and parts needed to build a circuit. They should conform to BS3939.
Schematics	Simple visual representations of circuit connections. There are different types of schematic: wiring, pneumatic and hydraulic. The wiring schematic displays the plan and function of a circuit. It shows where the components are connected, how the wires are connected and their location within the device.

Type of drawing	Description
	Pneumatic and hydraulic schematics represent the layout of valves (see Figure 3.1). Each box represents one position of the valve and shows how the fluid will flow through the valve in that position. 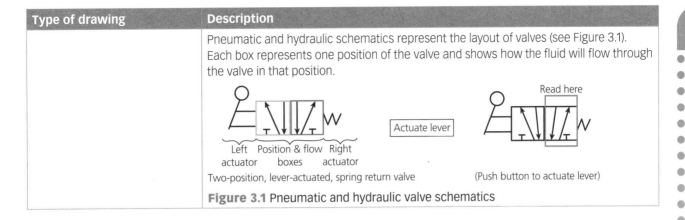

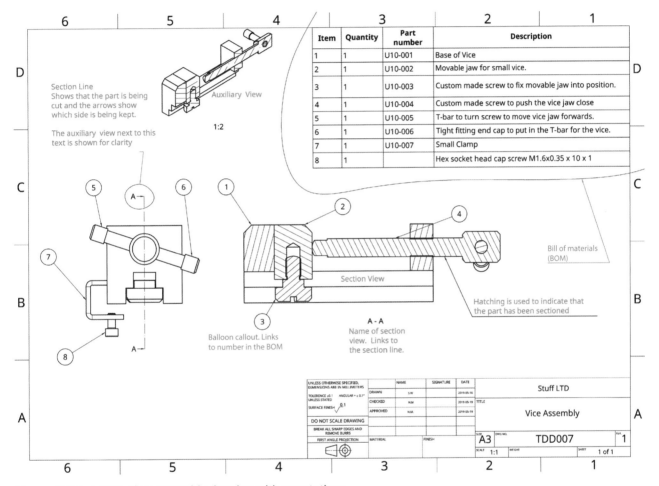

Figure 3.2 Example of an assembly drawing with annotations

Information displayed in engineering drawings

REVISED ○

Engineering drawings capture all necessary information in as few views as possible. If a component can be shown and detailed for manufacture in one view, then only one view should be used. Typically, three views are required for a complex shape. However, it may not always be obvious which is the 'front' or the 'top' and it is up to the engineer to select the views which show the details required for manufacture.

Engineering drawings display information in the format specified in BS 8888 *Technical product documentation and specification*. The type of drawing includes general assembly drawings (see Figure 3.2) that advise on how to fit components together to make a final piece, and detail drawings that concentrate on individual components and contain all the information needed for manufacture, including materials and dimensions. Both use orthographic projection to lay out information in a clear, readable way. For circuit diagrams, standard symbols are used as specified in BS 3939.

First and third angle

The two methods of laying out an orthographic drawing are first angle and third angle. They differ only in the way the views are shown. Each view shows the outlines of the shapes and features, and how they line up with each other.

The symbols in Figure 3.3 are used to state which projection is being used in the drawing. In first angle, the cone can be imagined on the top of the paper. It is then rotated to the left to show the side view. In third angle, imagine the cone is underneath some tracing paper, so it is rotated to the right to show the side view. This means that for first angle the views are reversed: the top of the part is on the bottom of the drawing, the bottom of the part on the top of the drawing, etc. (see Figure 3.4.) For third angle, the top of the part is shown at the top of the drawing (see Figure 3.5).

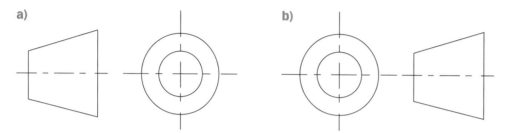

Figure 3.3 Graphical symbol for a) first angle and b) third angle orthographic projection

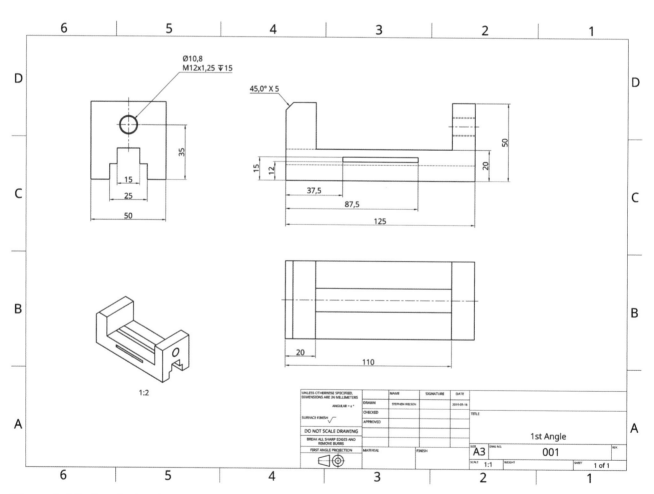

Figure 3.4 First angle drawing

Check your understanding and progress at **www.hoddereducation.co.uk/myrevisionnotes**

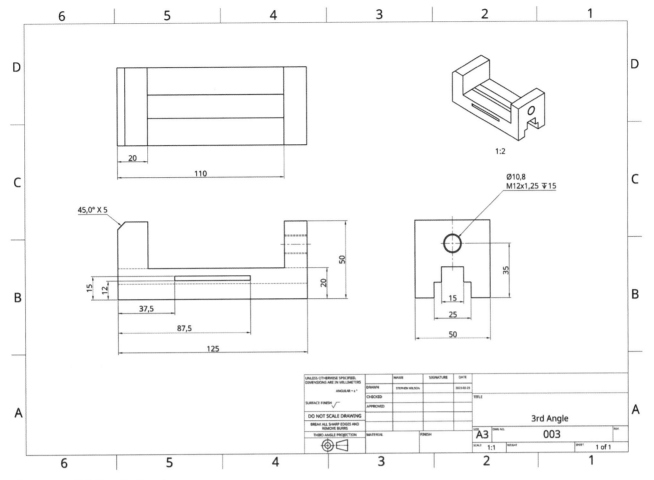

Figure 3.5 Third angle drawing

Title block

Some information within the title block is mandatory. The mandatory features include details of the legal owner, the creator and approver of the drawings, the document type, the document title and ID number, the date of issue and the sheet number (see Figure 3.6).

> **Title block** A title block should be displayed on every engineering drawing as it provides vital information about what the drawing contains and also an identification number (under which the drawing is officially filed).

Responsible department Engineering	Technical reference N. Makin	Document type Component drawing		Document status Released		
Legal owner C&G	**Created by** A. Buckenham	**Title** Mounting bracket	**Identification number** AB1211-4			
	Approved by S. Singh		**Rev.** A	**Date of issue** 2023-01-10	**Lang.** EN	**Sheet no.** 1/1

Figure 3.6 A typical title block layout

General arrangement (GA)

For larger projects the general arrangement will show an overview of what is to be provided. It will contain overall dimensions, contact details, drawing numbers for sub-assemblies and detail drawings, and references to design documents.

Section

A section view is a cut away of the object that allows the viewer to see what is happening inside a component. An example of this can be seen in the assembly drawing (Figure 3.2) above.

Auxiliary views and scale views

These are extra views which help to give clarity. These can be isometric views, partial sections, or a small area of the part shown at higher scale to capture some detail.

Abbreviations used in engineering drawings

Table 3.2 Abbreviations used in engineering drawings

Abbreviation	Meaning
AF	Across flats – the distance between two parallel faces of a nut
CL ﹣﹣．﹣．﹣	Centre line – centre lines are used to mark the centre of holes and to note lines of symmetry on a part
DIA or ø	Diameter – the diameter of a circle
R	Radius – usually used to show the radius of curves
MTL or MAT	Material – sometimes used on a note in the drawing
SQ	Square – for example, a square section on a round shaft
CHAM	Chamfer – where a small corner is taken off an edge
CSK	Countersunk/countersink – material removed at the top of a hole at an angle, usually to allow screws to sit flush
HEX	Hexagon head – a note on the type of bolt to be used
THD	Thread – the round and round bit of a screw
UCUT	Undercut – cutting a thin grove to the bottom of shaft
PCD	Pitch circle diameter – a way of dimensioning a number of holes at the same diameter around a circle
√ Ra 3.2	Surface finish symbol – this is how rough the surface finish is. Measured in micrometers (μm). Often checked using tactile gauges

Standard features in engineering drawings

Table 3.3 Standard features that can be found in engineering drawings

Feature	Standard representation
Internal screw thread	
External screw thread	

Feature	Standard representation
Nut	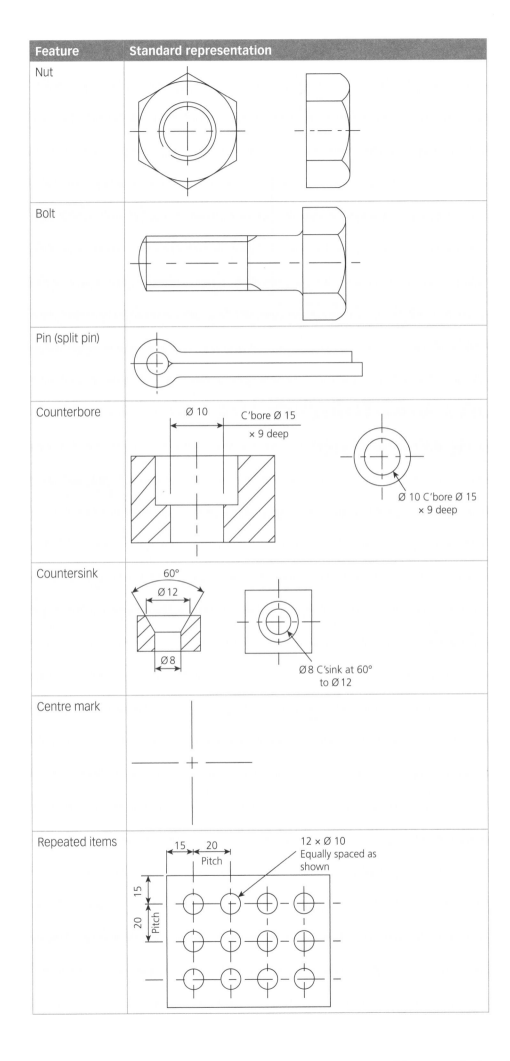
Bolt	
Pin (split pin)	
Counterbore	Ø 10 C'bore Ø 15 × 9 deep Ø 10 C'bore Ø 15 × 9 deep
Countersink	60° Ø 12 Ø 8 Ø 8 C'sink at 60° to Ø 12
Centre mark	
Repeated items	15 20 Pitch 15 20 Pitch 12 × Ø 10 Equally spaced as shown

My Revision Notes: Engineering and Manufacturing T Level

Revision activity

Figure 3.7 shows a part drawn in first angle. It is 30mm high, 50mm wide and 25mm deep. It has a 5mm chamfer and an M10 hole which is 20mm deep and 17mm of screwthread. The protrusion at the bottom is 15mm wide by 5mm deep.

Add the dimensions, centrelines and label the hole correctly. What is the position of the hole? How do you know? What does the part look like in three dimensions?

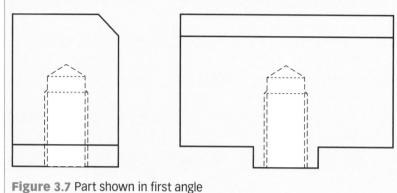

Figure 3.7 Part shown in first angle

3.2 Dimensions and tolerancing on engineering drawings

Dimensions

Dimensions are included on engineering drawings to show the measurements of features (see Figures 3.8 and 3.9).

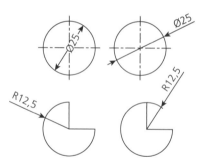

Figure 3.8 Example of radius and diameter dimensions

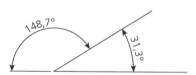

Figure 3.9 Angular dimensions

Exam tips

When dimensioning remember the following points.
+ Numbers are in the middle of the dimension: on the left of the line for vertical and above the line for horizontal.
+ Dimensions lines and numbers should be outside of the part.
+ There must be a small gap between extension lines and the part.
+ Small arrows must be placed at each end of the dimension line.
+ Units are not shown with dimensions, but will be stated in the title block on the drawing.

Tolerances

On the drawing there will be a general tolerance for all dimensions. If more accuracy is required, the required information will be stated next to the dimension. Tolerances can depend on how the part is dimensioned.

The tighter (smaller) the tolerance, the greater the cost.

Parallel dimensioning

The dimensions are shown from a datum and laid out in parallel (see Figure 3.10). This stops tolerances adding up across the part. If each dimension is ±1mm then the largest the part shown can be is 71mm and the smallest is 69mm.

> **Tolerance** The amount of variation allowed within the dimensions of a product or part being manufactured.
>
> **Datum** A face or edge or other feature from where all the measurements are taken.

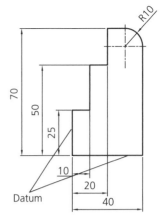

Figure 3.10 Part dimensioned using parallel dimensioning

Chain dimensioning

The dimensions follow on one from the other. Tolerances add up across the length of the part because each dimension is taken from the last. If each dimension is ±1mm then the largest the part can be is 73mm and the smallest is 67mm.

Table 3.4 shows how the vertical dimensions on the left of the drawing (Figure 3.11) add up from top to bottom.

Table 3.4 Vertical dimensions in Figure 3.11 from top to bottom

Vertical dim.	Max (+1/dim)	Min (–1/dim)	Max total	Min total
20	21	19	21	19
25	21 + 26	19 + 24	47	43
25	21 + 26 + 26	19 + 24 + 24	73	67

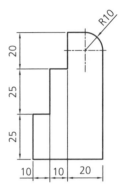

Figure 3.11 Part dimensioned using chain dimensioning

Limits and fits

There are a special set of tolerances for holes and shafts to ensure that a desired fit is produced. They are given special letter/number designations and can be looked up on a standard table. For example, a shaft DIA7 with a tolerance of f7 would be written DIA7f7 (or ⌀7f7) and would have a tolerance of –12 to –28μm.

Geometric dimensioning and tolerancing (GD&T)

GD&T is a way of describing the intent of the design. For example, a table may be within dimensional tolerance but the surface may not be flat. The required flatness of the table surface should be stated. A bolt through a thick piece of material requires that the hole should not be at an angle. The GD&T needs to state how perpendicular the hole should be to the top surface.

A feature control frame displays how to use GD&T and what it looks like. Figure 3.12 shows examples of the use of GD&T.

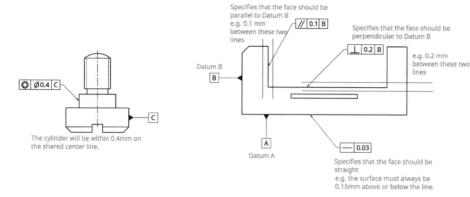

Figure 3.12 GD&T example

Now test yourself

1   Where might you use an isometric drawing instead of an orthographic one?
2   What is an advantage of parallel dimensioning?
3   What are the advantages of 3D modelling over hand drawing?
4   What is an assembly drawing for? What is a detail drawing for?
5   Describe how a schematic drawing represents a pneumatic valve.
6   How many views should be on an engineering drawing?
7   What are the standards for engineering drawing?

Summary

In this content area you learned about:
+ different styles of drawing that are needed to communicate different things to different people (engineers, managers, machinists, electricians, assemblers, pneumatic and hydraulic)
+ differences between first and third angle drawings
+ different ways of dimensioning drawings and the reasons for selecting one particular style
+ standard symbols and abbreviations used in engineering drawing.

Exam-style questions

1   What information would typically be included in a title block?   [2]
2   Sketch and explain three common line types used in an engineering drawing.   [2]
3   On a vertical line where would the dimension text be positioned?   [1]
4   What does the following symbol represent?   [1]

5   Describe the purpose of an assembly drawing.   [3]
6   What are the advantages to using GD&T over conventional dimensioning?   [4]
7   Explain why there are a special set of tolerances for holes and fits.   [3]
8   State why you might use a section view.   [1]
9   Evaluate the use of 3D CAD against hand drawing.   [4]

4 Essential mathematics for engineering and manufacturing

4.1 Applied mathematical theory in engineering applications

Standard arithmetic

Integers, decimals and standard form

Integers are whole numbers.

For example: –4, 0, 1, 3, 36, 209

Decimal numbers express fractions as a number of tenths, hundredths, thousandths, etc., stated after a decimal place.

For example: 1.2, 4.96, 4.897

Standard form is a notation used to express extremely large or extremely small numbers using a suffix in the form $\times 10^x$.

For example: $125\,000 = 1.25 \times 10^5$, $0.0000035 = 3.5 \times 10^{-6}$

Ordering

The acronym BIDMAS lists the order in which to carry out calculations:
+ Brackets
+ Indices (squares, square roots or other powers)
+ Division
+ Multiplication
+ Addition
+ Subtraction.

> **Integers** Whole numbers.
>
> **Decimal numbers** Express fractions as a number of tenths, hundredths, thousandths, etc., stated after a decimal place.
>
> **Standard form** Notation used to express extremely large or extremely small numbers using a suffix in the form $\times 10^x$.
>
> **BIDMAS** Defines the order in which to carry out calculations.

Worked example

Calculate:

$$a = (11 - 2) \times 12^2 + \frac{6}{3}$$

Answer

Carry out calculations in the following order

$$a = 9 \times 12^2 + \frac{6}{3}$$

$$a = 9 \times 144 + \frac{6}{3}$$

$$a = 9 \times 144 + 2$$

$$a = 1296 + 2$$

$$a = 1298$$

Decimal places and significant figures

The required resolution of decimal numbers is expressed in terms of decimal places (d.p.) or significant figures (s.f.).

✦ Decimal places specifies the required number of digits after the decimal place.

For example:

0.025 887 9 rounds up to 0.026 to 3 d.p.

1.364 78 rounds down to 1.36 to 3 d.p.

✦ Significant figures specifies the required number of digits not including any leading zeroes.

For example:

0.025 687 9 rounds up to 0.0257 to 3 s.f.

1.883 14 rounds down to 1.88 to 3 s.f.

Fractions, percentages, ratios and scale

Fractions are used to express proportions of a whole.

They are written in the form:

$$\frac{a}{b}$$

where a is the numerator, and b is the denominator.

The use and manipulation of fractions is achieved using the following rules.

Addition:

$$\frac{a}{b}+\frac{c}{d}=\frac{(a\times d)+(b\times c)}{b\times d}$$

Subtraction:

$$\frac{a}{b}-\frac{c}{d}=\frac{(a\times d)-(b\times c)}{b\times d}$$

Multiplication:

$$\frac{a}{b}\times\frac{c}{d}=\frac{a\times c}{b\times d}$$

Division:

$$\frac{a}{b}\div\frac{c}{d}=\frac{a}{b}\times\frac{d}{c}=\frac{a\times d}{b\times c}$$

Percentages (%) are used to express proportions of a whole as parts per hundred.

To express a number of parts, n, as a percentage of a total number of parts, N, use the formula:

$$\text{percentage (\%)} = \frac{n}{N}\times 100$$

Ratios are used to express the relationship between two or more quantities.

They are written in the form:

$a:b$ or $a:b:c$

Scale is a ratio that is used to express the difference in size between two quantities.

This is commonly used on engineering drawings. For example, an enlargement scale of 10:1 indicates that 10 units of distance on the drawing represents 1 unit of distance on the object being drawn.

Decimal places (d.p.)
Specifies the required number of digits after the decimal place.

Significant figures (s.f.)
Specifies the required number of digits not including any leading zeroes.

Fractions
Used to express proportions of a whole.

Percentages (%)
Used to express proportions of a whole as parts per hundred.

Ratios
Used to express the relationship between two or more quantities.

Scale
A ratio that is used to express the difference in size between two quantities.

Exam tips

Learn how to manipulate fractions as this makes rearranging complex formulae much easier.

Don't type long calculations into your calculator, break them down into stages using BIDMAS.

Now test yourself

TESTED ⬭

1 State the decimal number 0.002 359 to 2 s.f.

2 Calculate $\frac{3}{4}\div\frac{1}{3}$.

3 A batch of 60 components contains one defect. Calculate the number of defects as a percentage.

4 Concrete is mixed using cement, sand and gravel in the ratio 1:2:4.

You have 15 kg of cement. Calculate how much gravel you need to make concrete.

5 Using BIDMAS calculate: $\frac{14}{6}\times 9+3^2-6$

Typical mistake

Remember, when working with numbers in standard form, × 10^x are extremely large numbers and × 10^{-x} are extremely small numbers.

Check your understanding and progress at **www.hoddereducation.co.uk/myrevisionnotes**

Algebra

REVISED ○

Simplifying, factorising and manipulating equations

Algebra uses letters to represent the variables in an equation.

For example:

$$y = mx + c$$

Simplifying equations makes them easier to deal with and involves multiplying out, collecting like terms and identifying common factors so that an equation can be stated using as few terms as possible.

To simplify an algebraic equation you should:
+ multiply out any brackets
+ combine like terms
+ factorise by extracting common factors.

Worked example

Simplify the equation:

$$b = 3c(2 + 4a) - 2ac$$

Answer
+ multiply out the brackets
  $b = 6c + 12ac - 2ac$
+ combine like terms
  $b = 6c + 10ac$
+ factorise by extracting common factors
  $b = 2c(3 + 5a)$

Factorising involves the extraction of common factors and can be thought of as the opposite of multiplying out.

Manipulating or rearranging equations is a key skill in mathematics. The principal rule is that anything done to one side of an equation (on one side of an equals (=) sign) must also be done to the other.

Rearranging skills are required to change the subject of an equation. To do this use the following guidelines:
+ deal with anything affecting multiple terms such as squares, square roots (or other mathematical functions)
+ move the term containing the subject variable to the top line of the equation (if required)
+ isolate the term containing the subject variable (add or subtract the other terms)
+ isolate the subject variable (multiply or divide by numbers or other variables contained in the term containing the subject)
+ deal with squares, square roots (or other mathematical functions) affecting the subject variable.

Note that all these steps may not be required in every case.

Algebra Uses letters to represent the variables in an equation.

Variables Letters used to represent the values in an equation.

Simplifying equations Making them easier to deal with; involves multiplying out, collecting like terms, and identifying common factors so that an equation can be stated using as few terms as possible.

Terms Can be the numbers, single variables or products of variables and/or numbers that make up an equation.

Factorising This involves the extraction of common factors and can be thought of as the opposite of multiplying out.

Subject of an equation The unknown variable being calculated; appears on its own on one side of an equation.

Change the subject of the following equation to the variable u:

$$v = \sqrt{u^2 + 2as}$$

Answer

✦ eliminate the square root effecting multiple terms by squaring both sides of the equation

$$v^2 = u^2 + 2as$$

✦ isolate u^2 on one side of the equation by subtracting $2as$ from both sides

$$u^2 = v^2 - 2as$$

✦ isolate u by taking the square root of both sides of the equation

$$u = \sqrt{v^2 + 2as}$$

Simultaneous equations

Simultaneous equations are two or more equations that use the same variables and share at least one set of common solutions.

Graphical method

You can solve pairs of simultaneous linear equations graphically by plotting them on the same axes and finding where the lines intersect.

> **Simultaneous equations**
> Two or more equations that use the same variables and share at least one set of common solutions.
>
> **Linear equations** These have the standard form $y = mx + c$.

Worked example

Solve this pair of simultaneous equations using a graphical method:

$$y = 8x - 18$$

$$y = 2x + 3$$

Answer

✦ plot both graphs on the same axes
✦ find the (x, y) coordinates of the point where the lines intersect.

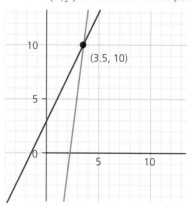

(3.5, 10)

Figure 4.1 Solving simultaneous equations graphically

In this example the graph shows that when $x = 3.5$ then $y = 10$ for both equations.

Analytical method 1: substitution

Substitution involves substituting one equation into another to make a third equation containing a single variable. This can then be solved.

Worked example

Solve this pair of simultaneous equations using substitution:

$$y = 8x - 18 \qquad (1)$$

$$y = 2x + 3 \qquad (2)$$

Answer

➕ substitute (2) into (1)

$$2x + 3 = 8x - 18 \qquad (3)$$

➕ simplify (3) to find x

$$3 + 18 = 8x - 2x$$

$$21 = 6x$$

$$x = \frac{21}{6}$$

$$x = 3.5$$

➕ substitute $x = 3.5$ into (1) to find y

$$y = 8 \times 3.5 - 18$$

$$y = 28 - 18$$

$$y = 10$$

Analytical method 2: elimination

Elimination involves adding or subtracting one equation from the other to make a third equation containing a single variable that can then be solved.

Worked example

Solve this pair of simultaneous equations using elimination:

$$y = 8x - 18 \qquad (1)$$

$$y = 2x + 3 \qquad (2)$$

Answer

➕ multiply (2) by 4 in order to make the x terms identical in both formulae.

$$4y = 8x + 12 \qquad (3)$$

➕ subtract (1) from (3)

$$4y = 8x + 12 \qquad (3)$$

$$y = 8x - 18 \qquad (1)$$

$$3y = 30 \qquad (4)$$

➕ simplify (4) to find y

$$y = \frac{30}{3}$$

$$y = 10$$

➕ substitute $y = 10$ into (1) to find x

$$10 = 8x - 18$$

$$8x = 28$$

$$x = 3.5$$

Quadratic equations

Quadratic equations have the standard form:

$$y = ax^2 + bx + c$$

To find the values of x when $y = 0$, called the roots of the equation, the equation must be stated in the form:

$$0 = ax + bx + c$$

The roots of a quadratic equation can be found graphically, by factorisation or by using the standard formula for solving quadratic equations.

Graphical method

You can solve a quadratic equation by plotting it on a graph. The roots of the equation are the values of x where the curve crosses the x-axis.

> **Worked example**
>
> Find the roots of this quadratic equation using the graphical method:
>
> $$y = x^2 - 2x - 8$$
>
> **Answer**
> + plot a graph of the quadratic equation
> + find the coordinates of the points where the curved line intersects with the x-axis
> + from the graph it can be seen that $y = 0$ when $x = -2$ or $x = 4$.
>
>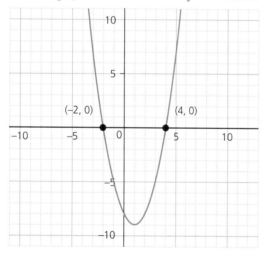
>
> **Figure 4.2** Solving a quadratic equation graphically

Factorisation method

The factorisation method starts with a quadratic equation rearranged into the form:

$$0 = ax^2 + bx + c$$

When $a = 1$, $0 = ax^2 + bx + c$ can be factorised into two brackets:

$$0 = (x + p)(x + q)$$

where $b = p + q$

and $c = pq$

Worked example

Find the roots of this quadratic equation using the factorisation method:

$$2 = x^2 - 2x - 6$$

Answer

+ rearrange into the standard form and equate to zero

$$0 = x^2 - 2x - 8$$

+ write the conditions that must be fulfilled by the values of p and q

$$-2 = p + q \text{ and } -8 = pq$$

+ by trial and error (or using simultaneous equations) find p and q

$$p = 2 \text{ and } q = -4$$

+ write the equation as the product of two factors

$$0 = (x + 2)(x - 4)$$

+ equate each factor to zero to find the corresponding values of x

when $(x + 2) = 0$ then $x = -2$

when $(x - 4) = 0$ then $x = 4$

Standard quadratic formula method

Quadratic equations with roots that are not integers can be solved using the quadratic formula.

Like the other methods we start with a quadratic equation rearranged into the form:

$$0 = ax^2 + bx + c$$

Roots can be calculated directly using the formula:

$$x = \frac{-b \pm \sqrt{b^2 - 4ac}}{2a}$$

Worked example

Find the roots of this quadratic equation using the formula method:

$$y = x^2 - 2x - 8$$

Answer

+ find the values of a, b and c by comparison with the standard form

$$a = 1$$
$$b = -2$$
$$c = -8$$

+ substitute these values into the formula

$$x = \frac{-(-2) \pm \sqrt{(-2)^2 - 4 \times 1 \times (-8)}}{2 \times 1}$$

$$x = \frac{2 \pm \sqrt{4 + 32}}{2}$$

$$x = \frac{2 \pm \sqrt{36}}{2}$$

$$x = \frac{2 \pm 6}{2}$$

+ calculate the roots directly

$$x = 4 \text{ and } x = -2$$

Indices

Indices are powers indicating the number of times a number or variable is multiplied by itself. Examples of the use of indices include familiar mathematical calculations such as those involving squares and square roots.

Indices Powers indicating the number of times a number or variable is multiplied by itself.

Logarithms (logs) Represent the power to which a given base must be raised to represent a given number and are often used when solving problems involving indices.

Table 4.1 The rules of indices

Operation	Rule	Example
Multiplication	$a^m \times a^n = a^{m+n}$	$a^2 \times a^3 = a^5$
Division	$\dfrac{a^m}{a^n} = a^{m-n}$	$\dfrac{a^4}{a^2} = a^2$
Powers	$(a^m)^n = a^{m \times n}$	$(a^2)^3 = a^6$

Table 4.2 Special cases involving indices

Index	Rule
$-n$	$a^{-n} = \dfrac{1}{a^n}$
$\dfrac{1}{2}$	$a^{\frac{1}{2}} = \sqrt{a}$
$\dfrac{1}{n}$	$a^{\frac{1}{n}} = \sqrt[n]{a}$
1	$a^1 = a$
0	$a^0 = 1$

Logarithms

Logarithms (logs) represent the power m to which a given base a must be raised to represent a number N. They are often used when solving problems involving indices.

Logs and indices are related and when

$$N = a^m$$

then

$$\log_a N = m$$

In engineering we usually encounter:

+ common logs which use base $a = 10$
+ natural logs which use base $a = e$ (where e is a mathematical constant known as Euler's number that is approximately equal to 2.718).

Table 4.3 The laws of logs

Operation	Common logs	Natural logs
	$\log_{10} N$ or $\log N$	$\log_e N$ or $\ln N$
Multiplication	$\log xy = \log x + \log y$	$\ln xy = \ln x + \ln y$
Division	$\log \dfrac{x}{y} = \log x - \log y$	$\ln \dfrac{x}{y} = \ln x - \ln y$
Powers	$\log x^n = n \log x$	$\ln x^n = n \ln x$

Table 4.4 Special cases involving logs

Common logs	Natural logs
$\log 0 =$ not defined	$\ln 0 =$ not defined
$\log 1 = 0$	$\ln 1 = 0$
$\log 10 = 1$	$\ln e = 1$

Worked example

Show that:

$$b = \log(a^2) + 2\log(ab)$$

can also be expressed as:

$$b = 4\log(a) + 2\log(b)$$

Answer

$$b = \log(a^2) + 2\log(ab)$$

➕ apply the power law

$$b = \log(a^2) + \log(ab)^2$$

➕ expand the brackets

$$b = \log(a^2) + \log(a^2b^2)$$

➕ apply the multiplication law

$$b = \log(a^2 a^2 b^2)$$

➕ gather like terms

$$b = \log(a^4 b^2)$$

➕ apply the multiplication law

$$b = \log(a^4) + \log(b^2)$$

➕ apply the power law

$$b = 4\log(a) + 2\log(b)$$

Determining numbers in a sequence

Arithmetic progression

An arithmetic progression is a sequence of numbers that takes the general form:

$$a_n = a + (n-1)d$$

Where:

a_n is the nth term in the sequence

a is the initial term in the sequence

d is the common difference between successive numbers in the sequence

n is the number of the term in the sequence.

For example, the following sequence shows the first five terms of an arithmetic progression where the initial term $a = 4$ and the common difference $d = 3$.

> **Arithmetic progression**
> Sequence of numbers that takes the general form:
> $$a_n = a + (n-1)d$$

4 Essential mathematics for engineering and manufacturing

4 Essential mathematics for engineering and manufacturing

n	1	2	3	4	5
Calculation	$4+(1-1)\times3$	$4+(2-1)\times3$	$4+(3-1)\times3$	$4+(4-1)\times3$	$4+(5-1)\times3$
a_n	4	7	10	13	16

Geometric progression

A geometric progression is a sequence of numbers that takes the general form:

$$a_n = ar^{n-1}$$

where:

a_n is the nth term in the sequence

a is the initial term in the sequence

r is the common ratio between successive terms in the sequence

n is the number of the term in the sequence.

For example, the following sequence shows the first five terms of a geometric progression where the initial term $a = 4$ and the common ratio $r = 3$:

n	1	2	3	4	5
Calculation	$4\times3^{1-1}$	$4\times3^{2-1}$	$4\times3^{3-1}$	$4\times3^{4-1}$	$4\times3^{5-1}$
a_n	4	12	36	108	324

Power series

A power series is an infinite series of terms that when added together can be used to approximate a given function. It has the general form:

$$\sum_{n=0}^{\infty} a_n (x-c)^n = a_0 + a_1(x-c) + a_2(x-c)^2 + \ldots$$

where:

$\sum_{n=0}^{\infty}$ indicates the sum of all terms between $n = 0$ and $n =$ infinity

x is a variable

c is a constant

a_n is the coefficient of the nth term in the sequence defined by a function independent of x.

n is the number of the term in the sequence.

> **Geometric progression** Sequence of numbers that takes the general form:
> $$a_n = ar^{n-1}$$
>
> **Power series** Infinite series of the form:
> $$\sum_{n=0}^{\infty} a_n (x-c)^n = a_0 + a_1(x-c) + a_2(x-c)^2 + \ldots$$

Typical mistake

When calculating logs make sure that you use the buttons on your calculator that correspond the base you are using and remember:

$$\log A = \log_{10} A$$

$$\ln A = \log_e A$$

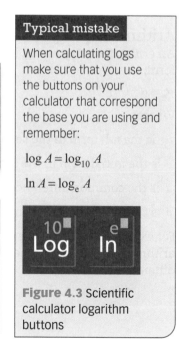

Figure 4.3 Scientific calculator logarithm buttons

Exam tips

Rearranging equations is an essential skill that you need to practice. Most maths-based exam questions will involve some algebraic manipulation.

When dealing with simultaneous equations or other multi-step processes, use a systematic approach. Use labels to identify the different equations and lay out your working clearly.

Refer to the formula sheet provided in the exam.

6   Solve this pair of simultaneous linear equations:

$y = 3x + 6$

$y = 6x + 9$

7   Find the roots of this quadratic equation:

$y = 2x^2 - 3x - 6$

8   Find x when:

$14 = 9^x$

9   Make v the subject of the equation:

$KE = \frac{1}{2}mv^2$

10   Calculate the 9th term in this geometric progression, given that the first term is 1.2.

$a_n = a \times 0.8^{n-1}$

Geometry

 REVISED ○

Table 4.5 Calculating the area of 2D shapes

2D shape	Area A of the shape
Square	$A = l^2$
Rectangle	$A = lw$
Triangle	$A = \frac{1}{2}bh$
Circle	$A = \pi r^2$ or $A = \frac{\pi D^2}{4}$

Table 4.6 Calculating the volume of 3D shapes

3D shape	Volume V of shape
Cube	$V = l^3$
Cuboid (or rectangular solid)	$V = lwh$
Cylinder	$V = \pi r^2 h$
Cone	$V = \pi r^2 \frac{h}{3}$

Calculus

 REVISED ○

Interpret and express changes in an engineering system from a graph

Calculus is a branch of mathematics that deals primarily with rates of change.

When plotted on a graph, linear equations form straight lines. The rate of change in a linear system is constant and can be calculated from the gradient of that line. The steeper the gradient, the greater the rate of change.

When plotted on a graph, non-linear equations are curves. The rate of change in a non-linear system varies. At any point on the curve the instantaneous rate of change can be calculated from the gradient of the tangent to the curve at that point.

Calculus A branch of mathematics that deals primarily with rates of change.

45

Straight-line graphs

Straight-line graphs represent linear systems described by equations with the standard form:

$$y = mx + c$$

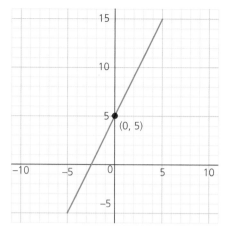

Figure 4.4 An example of a straight-line graph representing $y = 2x + 5$

Trigonometrical graphs

Repeating trigonometric waves represent systems described by equations of the standard form:

$$y = \sin x$$

$$y = \cos x$$

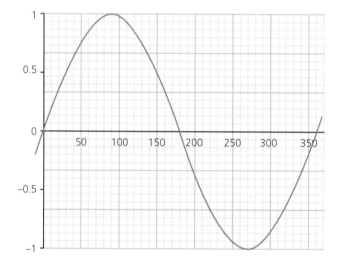

Figure 4.5 An example of a trigonometrical graph representing $y = \sin x$

Exponential graphs

Exponential curves represent systems described by equations of the standard form:

$$y = k^x$$

where k is a constant. These graphs always increase in the y-direction and never fall below the x-axis.

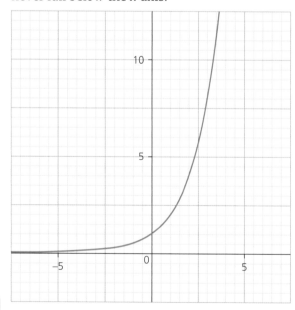

Figure 4.6 An example of an exponential graph representing $y = 2^x$

Check your understanding and progress at **www.hoddereducation.co.uk/myrevisionnotes**

Determining the equation of a straight line from a graph

A linear equation of the form $y = mx + c$ can be determined from a straight-line graph where:

m represents the gradient (slope) of the line in the equation

c is the value of y where the line intercepts the y-axis.

Worked example

Find the linear equation corresponding to the straight-line graph shown in Figure 4.7.

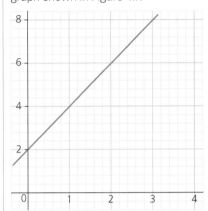

Figure 4.7 Graph representing an unknown linear equation

Answer

➕ calculate the gradient of the line

$$m = \frac{6}{3} = 2$$

➕ find the y-intercept

$$c = 2$$

➕ substitute these values into the standard form equation

$$y = 2x + 2$$

Determining standard differentials and integrals

Differentiation

For non-linear functions, differentiation can be used to calculate instantaneous rates of change. In other words, it can be used to find the gradient of the tangent to a curve at any point along its path.

> **Differentiation** Can be used to calculate instantaneous rates of change of a function.

Table 4.7 Standard derivatives

Function	Derivative
$y = a$ (where a is a constant)	$\frac{dy}{dx} = 0$
$y = x$	$\frac{dy}{dx} = 1$
$y = x^n$	$\frac{dy}{dx} = nx^{n-1}$
$y = ax^n$	$\frac{dy}{dx} = anx^{n-1}$
$y = e^x$	$\frac{dy}{dx} = e^x$
$y = e^{ax}$	$\frac{dy}{dx} = ae^{ax}$
$y = \sin ax$	$\frac{dy}{dx} = a\cos ax$
$y = \cos ax$	$\frac{dy}{dx} = -a\sin ax$
$y = \tan ax$	$\frac{dy}{dx} = a\sec^2 ax$

Calculate maximum and minimum values using differentiation

The maximum or minimum values of a function can be found by calculating the inflexion (or turning) points along its curve.

At an inflexion point, the instantaneous rate of change (i.e. the gradient of the curve) equals zero.

Quadratic equations have a single point of inflexion.

In this graphical example, you can see that for $y = x^2 - 2x + 3$ the inflexion point occurs when $y = 2$ and $x = 1$.

Differentiation can be used to calculate the inflexion point without drawing a graph.

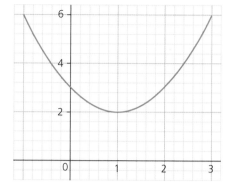

Figure 4.8 Quadratic equation with single point of inflexion

Worked example

Find the point of inflexion of this equation using differentiation:

$y = x^2 - 2x + 3$ (1)

Answer

✚ differentiate (1) to find the formula for instantaneous rate of change

$$\frac{dy}{dx} = 2x - 2$$

✚ equate to 0

$$0 = 2x - 2$$

✚ solve for x

$$x = 1$$

✚ to find y substitute $x = 1$ into equation (1)

$$y = 1^2 - 2 \times 1 + 3$$

✚ solve for y

$$y = 2$$

Integration

Integration is the reverse of differentiation.

Table 4.8 Standard integrals

Function	Indefinite integral
$y = a$ (where a is a constant)	$\int a \, dx = ax + C$
$y = x$	$\int x \, dx = \dfrac{x^2}{2} + C$
$y = ax^n$	$\int ax^n \, dx = \dfrac{ax^{n+1}}{n+1} + C$
$y = e^x$	$\int e^x \, dx = e^x + C$
$y = e^{ax}$	$\int e^{ax} \, dx = \dfrac{1}{a}e^{ax} + C$
$y = \sin x$	$\int \sin x \, dx = -\cos x + C$
$y = \sin ax$	$\int \sin ax \, dx = -\dfrac{1}{a}\cos ax + C$
$y = \cos x$	$\int \cos x \, dx = \sin x + C$

> **Integration** The reverse of differentiation.

> **Exam tip**
>
> In exams, marks are awarded for working so remember to write down every stage of a complex calculation.

> **Typical mistake**
>
> When integrating a function do not forget to add the unknown constant 'c'.

Check your understanding and progress at **www.hoddereducation.co.uk/myrevisionnotes**

11 Differentiate the following function with respect to x:

$y = 5x^2$

12 Differentiate the following function with respect to t:

$y = 5t^3 + t$

13 Differentiate the following function with respect to x:

$y = \tan(4x)$

14 Integrate the following function with respect to x:

$y = 15x^2 + 1$

15 Integrate the following function with respect to x:

$y = \sin(3x)$

Revision activity

Make flash cards for use when revising. This will help you to match up functions and their standard derivatives and integrals.

Trigonometry

Pythagoras' theorem and triangle measurement

Pythagoras' theorem states that 'for any right-angled triangle, the square of the hypotenuse is equal to the sum of the squares of the other two sides'.

That can be expressed mathematically as:

$a^2 = b^2 + c^2$

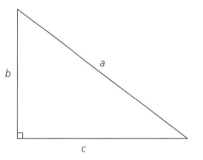

Figure 4.9 Application of Pythagoras' theorem to a right angled triangle

Table 4.9 Formulae used for circular measurements

2D shape	Area
Circumference	$C = 2\pi r$ or $C = \pi D$
Area	$A = \pi r^2$ or $A = \dfrac{\pi D^2}{4}$
Arc length*	Arc length $= r\theta$
Area of a sector*	Area of a sector $= \dfrac{1}{2} r^2 \theta$

*In calculations of arc length and area of a sector the angle θ must be stated in radians (where $360° = 2\pi$ radians).

Radians (rad) Unit of measure for angles commonly used in mathematics (2π rad = 360°)

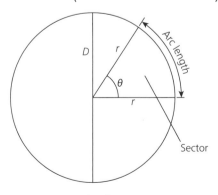

Figure 4.10 Circular measurements

49

Table 4.10 Formulae used for conversion between degrees and radians

Conversion	Formula
Degrees to radians	$\theta \text{ radians} = \theta° \times \dfrac{2\pi}{360}$
Radians to degrees	$\theta° = \theta \text{ radians} \times \dfrac{360}{2\pi}$

Table 4.11 Trigonometric functions

sine	$\sin\theta = \dfrac{\text{opp}}{\text{hyp}}$
cosine	$\cos\theta = \dfrac{\text{adj}}{\text{hyp}}$
tangent	$\tan\theta = \dfrac{\text{opp}}{\text{adj}}$

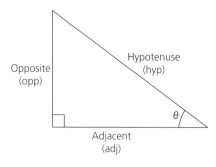

Figure 4.11 Application of trigonometry to a right angled triangle

Table 4.12 Common values of trigonometric functions

$\theta°$	θ radians	$\sin\theta$	$\cos\theta$	$\tan\theta$
0	0	0	1	0
30	$\dfrac{\pi}{6}$	$\dfrac{1}{2}$	$\dfrac{\sqrt{3}}{2}$	$\dfrac{1}{\sqrt{3}}$
45	$\dfrac{\pi}{4}$	$\dfrac{1}{\sqrt{2}}$	$\dfrac{1}{\sqrt{2}}$	1
60	$\dfrac{\pi}{3}$	$\dfrac{\sqrt{3}}{2}$	$\dfrac{1}{2}$	$\sqrt{3}$
90	$\dfrac{\pi}{2}$	1	0	n/a

Graphs of trigonometric functions

a)

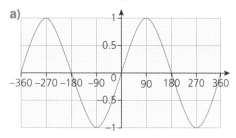

b)

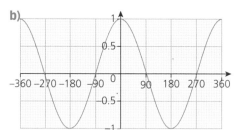

c)

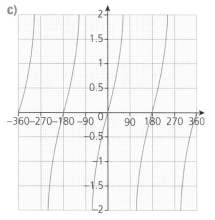

Figure 4.12 Graphs of trigonometric ratios a) $y = \sin\theta$ b) $y = \cos\theta$ c) $y = \tan\theta$

Check your understanding and progress at **www.hoddereducation.co.uk/myrevisionnotes**

Determining dimensions of a triangle using sine and cosine rules

The sine and cosine rules can be used to calculate angles and side lengths for triangles that do not contain a right angle (see Figure 4.13).

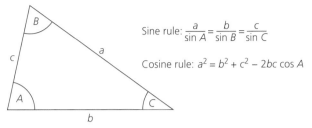

Sine rule: $\dfrac{a}{\sin A} = \dfrac{b}{\sin B} = \dfrac{c}{\sin C}$

Cosine rule: $a^2 = b^2 + c^2 - 2bc \cos A$

Figure 4.13 Sine and cosine rules

Common trigonometric identities

Table 4.13 Reciprocal trigonometric identities

Secant (sec)	$\sec\theta = \dfrac{1}{\cos\theta}$	$\sec\theta = \dfrac{\text{hyp}}{\text{adj}}$
Cosecant (csc)	$\csc\theta = \dfrac{1}{\sin\theta}$	$\csc\theta = \dfrac{\text{hyp}}{\text{opp}}$
Cotangent (cot)	$\cot\theta = \dfrac{1}{\tan\theta}$	$\cot\theta = \dfrac{\text{adj}}{\text{opp}}$

Table 4.14 Ratio trigonometric identities

$\tan\theta = \dfrac{\sin\theta}{\cos\theta}$
$\cot\theta = \dfrac{\cos\theta}{\sin\theta}$

> **Vector** Quantity fully defined by its magnitude, direction and sense.

Vectors and coordinates

Vector quantities are fully defined by their magnitude, direction and sense. Vectors commonly encountered in engineering include force, velocity and acceleration.

A vector $\overrightarrow{op}$ can be represented in polar form by a straight line where:
+ the magnitude is represented by the length of the line
+ the direction is indicated by the angle θ
+ the sense is indicated by the arrow.

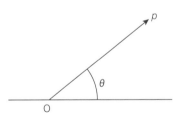

Figure 4.14 Vector $\overrightarrow{op}$ in polar form

Vectors can also be represented in cartesian form using:

$$\overrightarrow{op} = a\mathbf{i} + b\mathbf{j}$$

where a and b are the coordinates of the endpoint of the vector when plotted in an $(\mathbf{i}, \mathbf{j})$ coordinate system (see Figure 4.15).

Vectors can also be expressed as a column matrix using the notation $\begin{pmatrix} a \\ b \end{pmatrix}$.

The magnitude of vector $\overrightarrow{op}$ can be calculated using Pythagoras' theorem where

$$\left|\overrightarrow{op}\right| = \sqrt{a^2 + b^2}$$

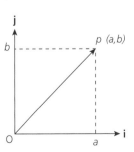

Figure 4.15 Vector $\overrightarrow{op}$ in cartesian form

Dot (or scalar) product

The dot (or scalar) product of two vectors gives a scalar quantity and can be thought of as directional multiplication.

Dot product can be expressed in several ways including:

$$(a\mathbf{i} + b\mathbf{j}) \times (c\mathbf{i} + d\mathbf{j}) = ac + bd$$

$$\begin{pmatrix} a \\ b \end{pmatrix} \cdot \begin{pmatrix} c \\ d \end{pmatrix} = ac + bd$$

$$\overrightarrow{op} \cdot \overrightarrow{oq} = |\overrightarrow{op}||\overrightarrow{oq}|\cos\theta$$

> **Dot (or scalar) product**
> Dot (or scalar) product of two vectors gives a scalar quantity and can be thought of as directional multiplication.

Worked example

Calculate the dot product of:

$$\overrightarrow{op} = 8\mathbf{i} + 3\mathbf{j}$$

$$\overrightarrow{oq} = 6\mathbf{i} + 1\mathbf{j}$$

Answer

✚ use the formula

$$(a\mathbf{i} + b\mathbf{j}) \cdot (c\mathbf{i} + d\mathbf{j}) = ac + bd$$

✚ substitute values for a, b, c, d

$$(8\mathbf{i} + 3\mathbf{j}) \cdot (6\mathbf{i} + 1\mathbf{j}) = (6 \times 8) + (3 \times 1)$$

✚ complete the calculation

$$48 + 3 = 51$$

You can then go on to calculate the angle between the vectors.

Worked example

Calculate the angle between $\overrightarrow{op}$ and $\overrightarrow{oq}$

Answer

✚ use the formula $\overrightarrow{op} \cdot \overrightarrow{oq} = |\overrightarrow{op}||\overrightarrow{oq}|\cos\theta$

✚ rearrange to make θ the subject

$$\theta = \cos^{-1}\left(\frac{\overrightarrow{op} \cdot \overrightarrow{oq}}{|\overrightarrow{op}||\overrightarrow{oq}|}\right) \qquad (1)$$

✚ calculate the magnitudes $|\overrightarrow{op}|$ and $|\overrightarrow{oq}|$

$$|\overrightarrow{op}| = \sqrt{8^2 + 3^2} = 8.544$$

$$|\overrightarrow{oq}| = \sqrt{6^2 + 1^2} = 6.083$$

✚ from the previous example we know that

$$\overrightarrow{op} \cdot \overrightarrow{oq} = 51$$

✚ substitute values into (1)

$$\theta = \cos^{-1}\left(\frac{51}{8.544 \times 6.083}\right)$$

✚ solve for θ

$$\theta = \cos^{-1}(0.981)$$

$$\theta = 11.2°$$

Cross (or vector) product

The cross (or vector) product of two vectors gives a vector perpendicular to the other two in three-dimensional space.

Cross product can be expressed in several ways including:

$$(a\mathbf{i}+b\mathbf{j}+c\mathbf{k})\times(d\mathbf{i}+e\mathbf{j}+f\mathbf{k})=(bf-ce)\mathbf{i}-(af-cd)\mathbf{j}+(ae-bd)\mathbf{k}$$

$$\overrightarrow{op}\times\overrightarrow{oq}=\left|\overrightarrow{op}\right|\left|\overrightarrow{oq}\right|\sin\theta$$

Scalars

Scalar quantities are fully defined by their magnitude. Commonly encountered scalars include mass, time and density.

Addition, subtraction and multiplication of matrices

Matrices are square or rectangular arrays of numbers commonly used to represent systems of simultaneous equations.

Each element in a matrix is represented by a lower-case letter with a subscript indicating its position in the matrix, e.g. a_{21} occupies a position in the second column, first row.

Addition of matrices

$$\begin{bmatrix} a_{11} & a_{21} \\ a_{12} & a_{22} \end{bmatrix}+\begin{bmatrix} b_{11} & b_{21} \\ b_{12} & b_{22} \end{bmatrix}=\begin{bmatrix} (a_{11}+b_{11}) & (a_{21}+b_{21}) \\ (a_{12}+b_{12}) & (a_{22}+b_{22}) \end{bmatrix}$$

Subtraction of matrices

$$\begin{bmatrix} a_{11} & a_{21} \\ a_{12} & a_{22} \end{bmatrix}-\begin{bmatrix} b_{11} & b_{21} \\ b_{12} & b_{22} \end{bmatrix}=\begin{bmatrix} (a_{11}-b_{11}) & (a_{21}-b_{21}) \\ (a_{12}-b_{12}) & (a_{22}-b_{22}) \end{bmatrix}$$

Multiplication of matrices

$$\begin{bmatrix} a_{11} & a_{21} \\ a_{12} & a_{22} \end{bmatrix}\times\begin{bmatrix} b_{11} & b_{21} \\ b_{12} & b_{22} \end{bmatrix}=\begin{bmatrix} (a_{11}b_{11})+(a_{21}b_{12}) & (a_{11}\times b_{21})+(a_{21}\times b_{22}) \\ (a_{12}b_{11})+(a_{22}b_{12}) & (a_{12}\times b_{21})+(a_{22}\times b_{22}) \end{bmatrix}$$

> **Now test yourself** TESTED ◯
>
> 16 Convert 270° into radians.
>
> 17 Use the cosine rule to find the length of side a shown in the diagram below.
>
>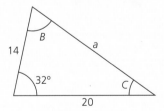
>
> 18 Find the magnitude of the vector:
>
> $$\overrightarrow{op}=\begin{pmatrix} 12 \\ 9 \end{pmatrix}$$
>
> 19 Multiply together these matrices:
>
> $$\begin{bmatrix} -2 & 3 \\ 9 & 4 \end{bmatrix}\quad\begin{bmatrix} 1 & 9 \\ 4 & -3 \end{bmatrix}$$
>
> 20 Calculate the dot product of these vectors:
>
> $$\begin{pmatrix} 8 \\ 1 \end{pmatrix}\begin{pmatrix} 7 \\ 2 \end{pmatrix}$$

Cross (or vector) product Cross or (vector) product of two vectors gives a vector perpendicular to the other two in three-dimensional space.

Scalar Quantity defined by its magnitude.

Matrices Square or rectangular arrays of numbers commonly used to represent vectors or systems of simultaneous equations.

> **Exam tip**
>
> Ensure that you know how to use all the main functions on your calculator including how to change the mode from Deg to Rad.

> **Typical mistake**
>
> When working with vectors and matrices it is very easy to make an arithmetic error so take your time and work methodically.
>
> When performing trigonometric calculations using radians, ensure your calculator is set to Rad mode.
>
>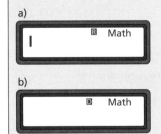
>
> **Figure 4.16** Typical calculator set to use a) radians b) degrees

Analysis of data and calculation of probabilities

Range is the difference between the highest and lowest number in a data set.

Cumulative frequency is the running total of the frequencies seen in a frequency distribution.

Measurements of central tendency (or averages) are known as mean, median and mode.

Mean $\bar{x}$ is the arithmetic average of the numbers in a data set calculated using the formula:

$$\bar{x} = \frac{x_1 + x_2 + x_3 + \ldots + x_n}{n}$$

Median is the central value in a data set arranged in order of increasing size.

For a data set with an odd number of values:

$$\text{median} = \left(\frac{n+1}{2}\right)\text{th term}$$

For a data set with an even number of values:

$$\text{Median} = \frac{\left(\frac{n}{2}\right)\text{th term} + \left(\frac{n}{2}+1\right)\text{th term}}{2}$$

Mode is the value that appears most frequently in a data set.

Standard deviation is a measure of variation about the mean and indicates how widely spread out the values in a data set are.

When considering all the values 'N' in a whole population, standard deviation σ is calculated using the formula:

$$\sigma = \sqrt{\frac{\sum(x - \bar{x})^2}{N}}$$

When standard deviation is calculated using a sample n of the data from a larger data set, the sample standard deviation s is calculated using the formula:

$$s = \sqrt{\frac{\sum(x - \bar{x})^2}{n-1}}$$

Determination of probabilities

Probability is used to measure the likelihood that an event will occur.

The probability that an event A will happen, $P(A)$, can be expressed as a fraction where:

$$P(A) = \frac{n_A}{N}$$

and where:

n_A is the number of instances of event A

N is the total number of events.

Estimation

Statistical estimation is a methodology used to estimate the characteristics of an entire population based on data from a relatively small random sample.

Sample mean and sample standard deviation are both statistical estimates. These are commonly used to analyse large populations where it is impractical to collect data on the whole population.

Check your understanding and progress at **www.hoddereducation.co.uk/myrevisionnotes**

Revision activity

Draw graphs of the trigonometric functions and label the x-axis using both degrees and radians expressed as fractions of π.

Range Difference between the highest and lowest number in a data set.

Cumulative frequency Running total of the frequencies seen in a frequency distribution.

Mean $\bar{x}$ Arithmetic average of the numbers in a data set.

Median Central value in a data set arranged in order of increasing size.

Mode Value that appears most frequently in a data set.

Standard deviation Measure of variation about the mean that indicates how widely spread out the values in a data set are.

Probability Used to measure the likelihood that an event will occur.

Exam tip

When calculating the standard deviation of a sample of data, organise your working into a table to help avoid making arithmetic errors.

4.2 Number systems used in engineering and manufacturing

Numbering systems

REVISED

Decimal numbers are expressed using base 10 and are written using the digits 0, 1, 2, 3, 4, 5, 6, 7, 8, 9. Table 4.15 shows how decimal numbers are built up using the sum of values expressed as powers of 10, for example 565 is made up of five 100s (10^2), six 10s (10^1) and five units (10^0).

Decimal numbers Numbers expressed using base 10.

Hexadecimal numbers Numbers expressed using base 16.

Binary numbers Numbers expressed using base 2.

Table 4.15 Decimal numbers in base 10 format

	10^5	10^4	10^3	10^2	10^1	10^0
	100000	10000	1000	100	10	1
27					2	7
565				5	6	5
10029		1	0	0	2	9

Hexadecimal numbers are expressed using base 16 and are written using digits 0, 1, 2, 3, 4, 5, 6, 7, 8, 9, A, B, C, D, E, F, G to represent the numbers 0 to 16. Table 4.16 shows how example decimal numbers are expressed as hexadecimal numbers built up using the sum of values expressed as powers of 16.

Table 4.16 Hexadecimal numbers in base 16 format

	16^5	16^4	16^3	16^2	16^1	16^0
	1048576	65536	4096	256	16	1
27					1	B
565				2	3	5
10029			2	7	2	D

Binary numbers are expressed using base 2 and are written using a combination of digits 0 and 1. Table 4.17 shows how example decimal numbers are expressed as binary numbers using the sum of values expressed as powers of 2.

Table 4.17 Binary numbers in base 2 format

	2^{13}	2^{12}	2^{11}	2^{10}	2^9	2^8	2^7	2^6	2^5	2^4	2^3	2^2	2^1	2^0
	8192	4096	2048	1024	512	256	128	64	32	16	8	4	2	1
27										1	1	0	1	1
565					1	0	0	0	1	1	0	1	0	1
10029	1	0	0	1	1	1	0	0	1	0	1	1	0	1

Applications of numbering in engineering and manufacturing

The decimal number system is by far the most common and is used throughout engineering as the basis for systems of measurement. For example, lengths, volumes and forces are all measured using decimal numbers.

Binary number systems have applications in computing where the digits 1 and 0 can be represented by the on and off states of an electrical signal.

Hexadecimal number systems are used in computer programming to reduce the need to enter long strings of binary numbers.

Now test yourself

21 Convert the hexadecimal number 2BF into a decimal number.

22 Convert the decimal number 19 into a binary number.

23 Calculate the range, mean, median and mode of the data set:

9, 10, 12, 13, 13, 14, 15, 16, 16, 17, 18, 21, 23, 24, 24, 24, 25

24 Calculate the median of this data set:

9, 10, 12, 13, 13, 14, 15, 16, 16, 17

25 Calculate the sample standard deviation of this sample from a data set:

14, 15, 16, 16, 17, 18, 21, 23

Revision activity

Collect your own set of data, such as the heights of your classmates, and conduct a statistical analysis to find the mean, median, mode and standard deviation.

Summary

In this content area you learned about:

+ arithmetic operations on integers, decimal numbers and numbers in standard form
+ using rules of arithmetical preference: brackets, indices, division, multiplication, adding and subtraction (BIDMAS)
+ working to a specified number of decimal places or significant figures
+ carrying out calculations using fractions, percentages, ratios and scale
+ simplifying, factorising and manipulating equations to change the subject
+ solving simultaneous and quadratic equations
+ applying rules of indices
+ applying laws of logarithms (base 10 and natural)
+ determining numbers in a sequence using arithmetic and geometric progression, power series
+ calculating the area of 2D shapes (square, rectangle, triangle, circle) and the volume of 3D shapes (cube, cuboid, cylinder, cone)
+ interpreting and expressing changes in an engineering system from a graph (straight-line, trigonometrical and exponential relationships)

+ determining the equation of a straight line from a graph ($y = mx + c$).
+ determining standard differentials and integrals (basic arithmetic operations, powers/indices, trigonometric functions)
+ calculating maximum and minimum values using differentiation
+ using Pythagoras' theorem and triangle measurement
+ circular measure and converting between radians and degrees
+ applications of trigonometric functions (sin, cos, tan), their common values, rules and graphical representation
+ determining dimensions of a triangle using sine and cosine rules
+ using common trigonometric identities (sec, csc, cot)
+ using vectors including addition, dot and cross product
+ addition, subtraction and multiplication of matrices
+ calculation of range, cumulative frequency, averages (mean, median and mode) and standard deviation for statistical data
+ calculating probabilities in practical engineering situations.

Exam-style questions

1 The shape in Figure 4.18 must be accurately measured before manufacturing.
 Calculate the length of the side LM. [3]

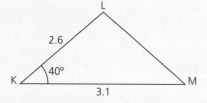

Figure 4.18 Non-right angled triangle (not to scale)

2 Concrete consists of cement, sand and aggregate mixed by weight in the ratio 1 : 2 : 4.
 A batch of dry mix weighs 28 kg in total.
 Calculate the weight of sand used in the mix. [3]

3 In the first week of production of a new product, four defective parts were identified during quality inspection. In the second week, 12 defective parts were identified. In the third week, 36 defective parts were identified.

Use your knowledge of geometric progression to predict the number of defects that can be expected in week four. [3]

4 A random sample of 506 component parts were selected for inspection. It was found that nine of these components had defects.

Calculate the probability that a component selected at random would be defect free and state your answer to 3 s.f. [3]

5 An electronic circuit is designed to change the amplitude of an incoming signal.

The action of the circuit is be represented by the equation:

$$A = \frac{a^3}{a^{-\frac{1}{2}}} \times a^{-\frac{3}{2}}$$

where a is the amplitude of the input signal and A is the amplitude of the output signal.

Determine the simplest form of the equation that represents the action of the circuit. [2]

6 The height of a projectile fired vertically upwards is described by the equation:

$$h = 30t - 4.905t^2$$

where h is the height of the projectile in m and t is time in s.

Determine the values of t for which $h = 15\,\text{m}$. [3]

7 The current flowing in two branches of an electrical circuit are described by the equations:

$$3I_1 - 2I_2 = 5$$
$$4I_1 + 5I_2 = 12$$

Determine the values of I_1 and I_2. [3]

8 The distance between a tool and a fixed point on a machine is described by the function:

$$d = 3\sin(2t) + 5$$

Where d is the distance from a fixed point in mm and t is time in s.

Determine the velocity of the tool when $t = 2\,\text{s}$. [4]

9 A digital signal processor uses binary data represented in hexadecimal form.
   a Convert the decimal number 456 into binary form. [1]
   b Convert the decimal number 456 into hexadecimal form. [1]

10 A civil engineer is conducting a study of the compressive strength of concrete samples. They have collected a set of ten measurements in MPa:

15.2, 16.7, 18.1, 17.5, 14.9, 16.3, 15.8, 17.2, 16.5, 15.7

Determine the standard deviation for this data set. [3]

5 Essential science for engineering and manufacturing

5.1 Units of measurement used in engineering

+ Units of measurement allow engineering parameters to be quantified.
+ SI (metric) units are an agreed international standard for measuring, split into base and derived units.
+ Derived units are a combination of different base units.

SI (metric) units Units that are part of an agreed international standard for measuring.

Multiples The factors used to create larger forms of SI units.

Submultiples The factors used to create smaller forms of SI units.

Table 5.1 SI base units

Quantity	SI base unit
Length	metre (m)
Mass	kilogram (kg)
Time	second (s)
Electric current	ampere (A)
Thermodynamic temperature	kelvin (K)

Table 5.2 SI derived units

Quantity	SI derived unit
Acceleration	metres per second squared ($m\,s^{-2}$)
Density	mass per unit volume ($kg\,m^{-3}$)
Force	Newton (N)
Pressure	Pascal (Pa) or $N\,m^{-2}$
Torque	Newton metre (N m)
Velocity	metres per second ($m\,s^{-1}$)
Volume	cubic metre (m^3)
Area	square metre (m^2)

+ Multiples are the factors used to create larger forms of SI units. Submultiples are used to make smaller forms.

Table 5.3 Examples of multiples

Prefix	Symbol	Number	Factor
Kilo	k	1000	10^3
Mega	M	1000000	10^6
Giga	G	1000000000	10^9
Tera	T	1000000000000	10^{12}

Table 5.4 Examples of submultiples

Prefix	Symbol	Number	Factor
Milli	m	0.001	10^{-3}
Micro	μ	0.000001	10^{-6}
Nano	n	0.000000001	10^{-9}
Pico	ρ	0.000000000001	10^{-12}

✦ The imperial system of measurement has not been officially used in the UK since 1965, but some countries, such as the USA, still use it. Therefore it is important to be able to convert between imperial and metric units.

Imperial (units) Units that are part of the imperial system.

Table 5.5 Conversion factors for imperial to SI units

Length	1 inch = 2.54 centimetres
	1 foot = 30.48 centimetres
	1 yard = 91.44 centimetres
Volume	1 fluid ounce = 28.41 millilitres
	1 gallon = 4.55 litres
Mass	1 ounce = 28.35 grams

Exam tip

Make sure you know the difference between SI and imperial units, and how to convert between them.

Now test yourself   TESTED ⬤

1 What is the SI derived unit for velocity?
2 What parameter is measured in ounces?
3 Convert 2 yards into centimetres.

Revision activity

Play a mix-and-match game with the SI units shown in the tables above. You could do this by creating flashcards and testing yourself or fellow students.

5.2 Vector and coordinate measuring systems

✦ Vector quantities have both magnitude and direction. Examples include:
  ✦ displacement, which is the change in position of an object
  ✦ velocity, which is the speed at which an object moves in a particular direction
  ✦ acceleration, which is the rate at which velocity changes.
✦ Scalar quantities have magnitude, but no direction. Examples include:
  ✦ distance, which is how far an object moves
  ✦ speed, which is the rate at which an object moves over a certain distance.

Vector quantity A quantity with both magnitude and direction.

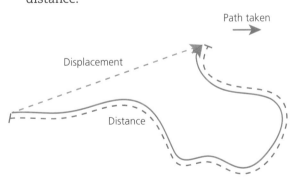

Figure 5.1 Displacement measures the change in position of an object

Polar and Cartesian coordinates

+ Polar coordinates are used to determine the location of a point on a plane in terms of the distance from a reference point (r) and the angle from a reference direction (θ). The points are plotted as (r, θ).
+ Cartesian coordinates are used to specify the distances of a point from the coordinate axes on a graph. Depending on whether they are being expressed in two or three dimensions, the points are plotted as either (x, y) or (x, y, z).

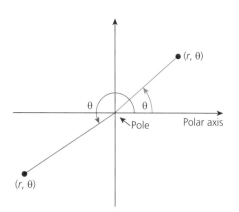

Figure 5.2 The polar coordinate system

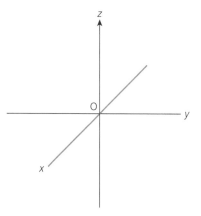

Figure 5.3 The Cartesian coordinate system is made up of three mutually perpendicular coordinate axes

> **Polar coordinates** A system that is used to determine the location of a point on a plane in terms of the distance from a reference point (r) and the angle from a reference direction (θ).
>
> **Cartesian coordinates** A system that is used to specify the distances of a point from the coordinate axes on a graph.

Converting between polar and Cartesian coordinates

It is possible to convert between Cartesian and polar coordinates, where the angles are in degrees.

To convert Cartesian coordinates into polar coordinates:

$$r = \sqrt{x^2 + y^2}$$

$$\theta = \tan^{-1}\frac{y}{x}$$

To convert polar coordinates into Cartesian coordinates:

$$x = r\cos\theta$$

$$y = r\sin\theta$$

> **Exam tip**
>
> Make sure you can convert from polar to Cartesian coordinates, and vice versa.

> **Now test yourself**
>
> 4 What type of quantity has both magnitude and direction?
>
> 5 How are polar coordinates represented?
>
> TESTED ◯

5.3 Scientific methods and approaches to scientific inquiry and research

The steps of the scientific method

REVISED ◯

+ Make an observation and ask a question that needs to be answered.
+ Gather background information and complete research, for example previous studies or equipment that may need to be used.
+ Form a hypothesis (a testable statement of the expected outcome of a study).
+ Create a prediction/simulation, and test the hypothesis through conducting experiments and gathering formal data.
+ Analyse the results and form a conclusion: do the results support the initial hypothesis?

> **Scientific method** A series of steps that provides a systematic and objective approach to acquiring knowledge.
>
> **Hypothesis** A testable statement of the expected outcome of a study.

+ Share the results and consider a further hypothesis (iteration) if the results are not proven (see Figure 5.4).

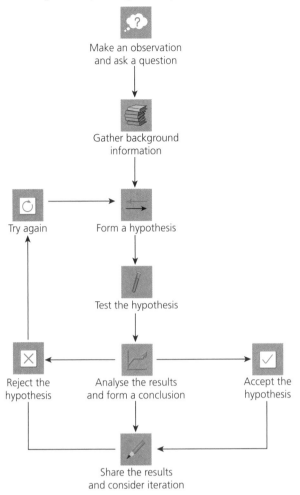

Make an observation
and ask a question

Gather background
information

Try again

Form a hypothesis

Test the hypothesis

Reject the
hypothesis

Analyse the results
and form a conclusion

Accept the
hypothesis

Share the results
and consider iteration

Figure 5.4 Steps of the scientific method

Iteration A further hypothesis if the results of the initial hypothesis are not proven.

Exam tip

Make sure you can describe each step of the scientific method.

Now test yourself

6 State what is meant by the scientific method.

7 What is the purpose of testing within the scientific method?

TESTED

Revision activity

Ask a question about the performance of a process or a piece of equipment. For example, why is it not performing at optimum efficiency? Use the scientific method to investigate this question and form a conclusion as to why it is happening.

5.4 Measurement equipment, techniques and principles

Measurement principles

REVISED

+ Accuracy is how close a measurement is to a known standard.
+ Precision is how close measurements are to each other, or how repeatable they are.
+ Uncertainty is the margin of doubt about a measurement. This is quantified by the width of the margin and a percentage confidence level.
+ Resolution is the smallest increment or decrement that can be shown as a result of measurement.
+ Tolerance is the acceptable limits in variation of a measurement. For example, there might be a tolerance of ±2mm for the length of a part.
+ Calibration ensures that measurement equipment produces measurements that are accurate and repeatable.

Accuracy How close a measurement is to a known standard.

Tolerance The amount of variation allowed within the dimensions of a product or part being manufactured.

Measurement equipment

REVISED

+ Rules are used to measure linear distance. They are straightforward to use, but their accuracy is limited to 1mm or 0.5mm, depending on how they are marked.

+ Vernier callipers are measurement devices accurate to 0.01 mm (see Figure 5.5). They can be used to measure external and internal dimensions, or the depth of the inside of an object. Digital callipers display the results of measurement on a digital screen, so do not require interpretation of the Vernier scale.
+ Micrometers are accurate to 0.001 mm. Inside micrometers measure internal dimensions, outside micrometers measure external dimensions and depth micrometers measure the depth of holes and bores.
+ Angle gauges provide a template for measuring angles between different lines or surfaces.
+ Slip gauges measure gaps or space between parts through the use of machined blocks. They are very accurate and easy to use. They can even be used to verify the accuracy of other measurement equipment.
+ Go/no-go gauges are used to check the lower (go) and upper (no-go) tolerance limits of features in a product.
+ Dial test indicators (DTIs) are used to measure flatness and roundness, showing the results on the dial face.
+ A coordinate measuring machine (CMM) is an automated piece of measuring equipment that measures the three-dimensional geometry of an object.

> **Vernier callipers** Devices that can be used to measure internal, external or depth measurements using the Vernier scale.
>
> **Micrometers** Very accurate measurement devices that come in different forms depending on the measurements being taken – inside, outside and depth.

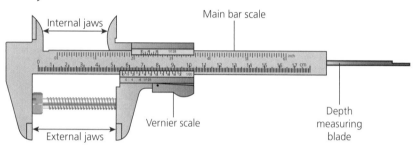

Figure 5.5 Vernier calliper

Now test yourself   TESTED ◯

8 What is meant by the accuracy of a measurement?
9 How accurate are Vernier callipers?

> **Typical mistake**
>
> It is easy to mix up the functions of the different types of micrometer. Make sure you know what each is used to measure.

Revision activity

Practice using the different measuring equipment to measure appropriate parameters. Explain how each was used and the benefits and limitations of each.

5.5 Chemical composition and behaviours

Chemical composition   REVISED ◯

Atomic structure

+ Atoms consist of a central nucleus, surrounded by one or more negatively charged electrons (see Figure 5.6). An atom is typically around 100 picometers (1×10^{-10} m) in size. Electrons are negatively charged particles.
+ The nucleus contain protons and neutrons. Protons are positively charged particles whereas neutrons have no electric charge.
+ The valence of the atomic structure is the number of bonds that its atoms can form with other atoms. The valence shell is the outermost electron shell of an atom.
+ Atoms can be combined to form molecules.
+ An element cannot be broken down any further – it is a single type of atom. If atoms contain an electric charge, they are known as ions.

> **Atom** The smallest unit into which matter can be divided without the release of charged particles.
>
> **Electrons** Negatively charged particles.
>
> **Protons** Positively charged particles.

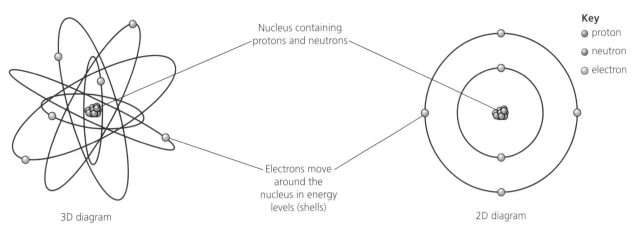

Key
● proton
● neutron
● electron

Nucleus containing protons and neutrons

Electrons move around the nucleus in energy levels (shells)

3D diagram

2D diagram

Figure 5.6 Atomic structure

Chemical structure

✚ Solutions are homogenous mixtures (mixtures that become uniform in structure, e.g. salt dissolving into water) formed by combining two or more substances.
✚ Suspensions are heterogenous mixtures (mixtures that are composed of many separate parts, e.g. a bowl of cereal and milk) formed by the mixing of solid particles in liquid without dissolving.
✚ Solubility is the degree to which a chemical dissolves in water.
✚ A compound is a substance made from two or more elements that are bonded together, and therefore difficult to separate.
✚ A mixture is formed by combining two or more chemical substances. These are not permanently bonded.
✚ The periodic table shows the different chemical elements in a clear, tabular format. The elements are listed in rows in order of increasing atomic number. Elements with similar properties are grouped together in columns.

> **Solutions** Homogenous mixtures formed by combining two or more substances.

Behaviours

REVISED ⬤

Chemicals in electricity

✚ Cells change chemical energy into electrical energy. Two or more cells can be joined together to create a battery.
✚ Primary cells cannot be recharged, whereas secondary cells can.
✚ Cell capacity is the amount of charge that the cell can deliver.
✚ Power capacity is the maximum power output of a generator.
✚ Internal resistance is the opposition to the flow of current produced in a cell or battery.

Electrolysis

✚ Electrolysis is the use of electricity to break down ionic compounds.
✚ Anodes are positive electrodes. Cathodes are negative electrodes. These are connected to an electrical power supply and placed into an electrolyte (a medium containing ions).
✚ The negatively charged ions (anions) are attracted towards the anode and positively charged ions (cations) are attracted towards the cathode.
✚ Plating is a finishing process whereby electrolysis is used to deposit a metal on the surface of material, protecting it from wear and corrosion.
✚ Galvanic protection is a corrosion-protection method that uses an electrolytic reaction to coat a metal with a more reactive metal.
✚ Dissociation is the process of breaking up a compound into simpler components that could, under other conditions, recombine.

> **Electrolysis** The use of electricity to break down ionic compounds.

Reactions of metals and alloys

+ When metals react with acid it produces salt and hydrogen.
+ This also occurs when some metals react with alkalis (chemicals that make acids less acidic).
+ Some metals are more reactive than others, e.g. gold is less reactive than sodium.
+ One process that uses these types of reactions to create markings on metal is chemical etching.

> **Now test yourself** TESTED ⬤
>
> 10 What do atoms consist of?
> 11 What is produced when metals react with acids?

5.6 Forces and motion in engineering

Types of motion

+ **Rotary motion** is motion in a circle, for example the turning of a wheel (see Figure 5.7).
+ **Linear motion** is motion in a straight line, such as a train moving along a straight track.
+ **Reciprocating motion** is motion that moves back and forth in a straight line, for example the action of a piston in an internal combustion engine.
+ **Oscillating motion** is motion that moves back and forth about a pivot, for example the swinging of a clock pendulum.

Rotary motion Circular motion.

Linear motion Motion in a straight line.

Reciprocating motion Motion that moves back and forth in a straight line.

Oscillating motion Motion that moves back and forth about a pivot.

Torque The force that causes an object to rotate about an axis. It is measured in newton-metres (Nm).

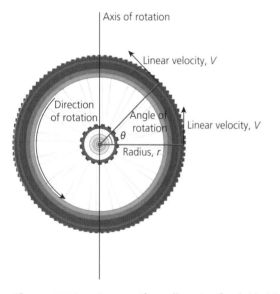

Figure 5.7 In rotary motion, all parts of a rigid object move in circular orbits around a common axis with the same angular velocity

Forces

+ Pressure (p) is the force (F) applied perpendicular to the surface of an object, per unit area (A) that the force is distributed, measured in pascals (Pa). It is represented by the formula, $p = \dfrac{F}{A}$.

+ Forces are vector quantities because they have both magnitude and direction. Vector forces are typically represented using scaled vector diagrams.

+ Balanced forces are forces that are equal in size but act in opposite directions.

- With unbalanced forces, the force applied in one direction is greater than the force applied in the opposite direction.
- A moment is the turning effect of a force. The size of a moment (M) can be calculated by multiplying the force (F) by the perpendicular distance from the pivot to the line of action of the force (d) using the formula $M = F \times d$.
- Torque is the force that makes an object rotate about an axis. It is measured in newton-metres (Nm).
- Equilibrium occurs when the sum of the forces acting on an object is zero, or the sum of the torque acting on an object is zero.
- Co-planar forces are forces that all act in one plane.

> **Exam tip**
>
> Ensure you can perform calculations using the formulae for pressure and moments. Always show all of your working.

Now test yourself TESTED ◯

12 What is motion that moves back and forth about a pivot called?

13 What is the formula for pressure?

> **Revision activity**
>
> Research engineering applications of each of the different types of motion. Present your findings as a mind map.

5.7 Fluid dynamics in engineering

Fluid dynamics REVISED ◯

- Hydrostatic pressure is the pressure exerted by a height h of fluid (water or liquid) of density ρ on a surface. It can be calculated using the formula for pressure p

  $p = \rho \times g \times h$, where g is the acceleration due to gravity

- Hydrostatic thrust: a force acting on a surface that is submerged in a liquid. The thrust force (F) can be calculated using the formula

  $F = \rho \times g \times h \times A$, where A is the area of submerged surface in m^2

- The centre of pressure is the point at which the total amount of pressure acts on a body.
- Viscosity is the measurement of a fluid's resistance to flow, measured in Nsm^{-2}.
- Bernoulli's principle states that as the speed of a fluid increases, the pressure within the fluid decreases. This principle explains how aircraft wings work. When the air flowing past the top surface of the wing is moving more quickly than the air moving past the bottom surface, the pressure below the wing will be higher. This creates upwards lift.

Flow characteristics around a two-dimensional shape

- Laminar flow is fluid flow that occurs in parallel layers with no mixing.
- Turbulent flow is when fluid particles start to mix in a zig-zag pattern, resulting in significant loss of energy.
- Vortices are regions of fluid flow that resemble whirlpools. The flow revolves around an axis line.
- Separation points occur where the boundary layer detaches from a surface to form a wake, or turbulent flow.

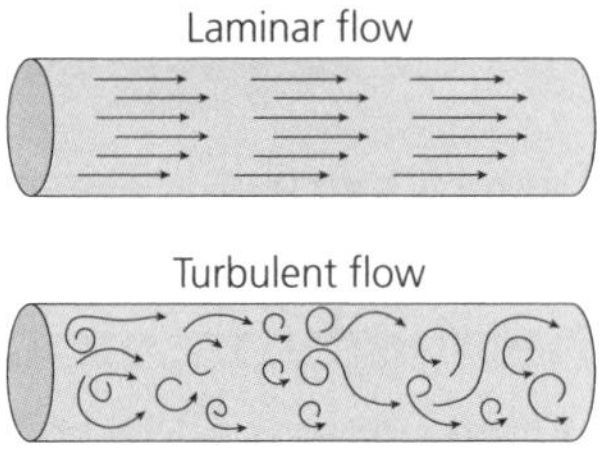

> **Hydrostatic pressure** The pressure exerted by water or liquid on a surface.
>
> **Viscosity** The measurement of a fluid's resistance to flow.
>
> **Laminar flow** Smooth fluid flow that occurs in parallel layers with no mixing.
>
> **Turbulent flow** Flow where fluid particles start to mix in a zig-zag pattern.

Laminar flow

Turbulent flow

Figure 5.8 Laminar and turbulent flows

Principles of aerodynamics

+ Aerodynamics is the study of how objects move through the air.
+ Drag is the resistance force of the air, opposing the movement of the object through it.
+ Thrust is the force that enables an object to move forward through the air, overcoming drag.
+ Lift is the upwards force that opposes gravity and enables aircraft to fly.

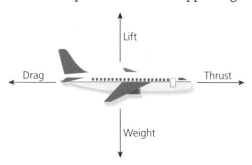

Figure 5.9 Aerodynamic principles

Now test yourself   TESTED ⬤

14 What does Bernoulli's principle state?
15 What is the aerodynamic force that opposes the forwards movement of an object through the air?

5.8 Thermodynamics in engineering

Heat transfer mechanisms

+ Conduction is the transfer of heat through the direct contact between objects.
+ Convection is the transfer of heat through movement of particles in liquids or gases.
+ Radiation is the transfer of heat via electromagnetic waves.

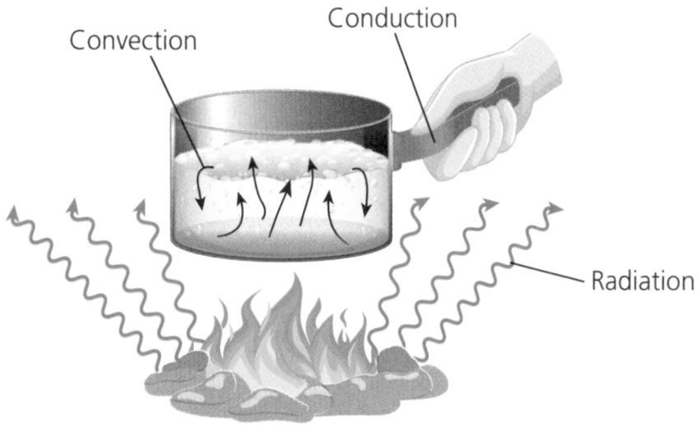

Convection   Conduction

Radiation

Figure 5.10 Heat transfer mechanisms

Thermodynamic systems

+ Open systems allow both mass and energy transfer to take place.
+ Closed systems allow energy transfer to take place but mass remains constant.
+ The temperature of a substance is directly proportional to the average kinetic energy of the particles in that substance.
+ Pressure is the force applied perpendicular to the surface of an object, per unit area that the force is distributed.
+ The volume of an object is the amount of three-dimensional space occupied by that object.

Types of heat

+ Sensible heat is heat added to or removed from a substance that causes a change in its temperature but does not cause a change in its state.
+ Latent heat is heat added to or removed from a substance that does not cause a change in its temperature but does cause a change in its state. The latent heat of fusion of a substance is the amount of energy needed for that substance to change its state from solid to liquid, and the latent heat of evaporation is the amount of heat needed to change its state from liquid to gas.

The equation for sensible heat is:

$$Qm = c\Delta t$$

where Q is the amount of heat energy, m is mass, c is heat capacity and Δt describes the temperature change.

The equation for latent heat is:

$$Qm = h$$

where Q is the amount of heat energy, m is mass and h is specific latent heat.

Latent heat Heat added to or removed from a substance that does not cause a change in its temperature but does cause a change in its state, for example from solid to liquid.

Expansivity and coefficient of heat transfer

+ Expansivity is how much a material expands or contracts due to a temperature change of one degree.
+ The coefficient of heat transfer shows how well heat energy transfers from one resistant material to another.

Thermodynamic equations

+ Absolute temperature $T = t + 273.15$, where t is temperature in °C.
+ Absolute pressure $P_{abs} = P_g$ (gauge pressure) $+ P_{atm}$ (atmospheric pressure)
+ Density $\rho = \dfrac{m}{V}$, where m is the mass of the object and V is its volume.
+ Boyle's law (the relationship between pressure and temperature of an ideal gas) states that

$$p_1 V_1 = p2V2$$

where p_1 is the initial pressure, V_1 is the initial volume, p_2 is the final pressure and V_2 is the final volume (see Figure 5.11).

+ Charles' law states that $\dfrac{V_1}{T_1} = \dfrac{V_2}{T_2}$
+ The general gas equation states that $\dfrac{pV}{T} = $ constant
+ The characteristic gas equation states that that $pV = mRT$ where R is a characteristic gas constant and m is number of moles of gas.

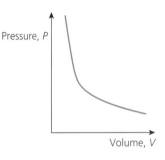

Pressure, P

Volume, V

Figure 5.11 Boyle's law

Typical mistake

Remember that to calculate absolute temperature you must add 273.15 to the temperature measured in degrees Celsius.

Now test yourself

TESTED ⬤

16 What is the transfer of heat via electromagnetic waves called?
17 What does the characteristic gas equation state?

Summary

In this content area you learned about:

+ the SI and imperial units used in engineering and how to convert between them
+ the differences between scalar and vector coordinates
+ how to convert between Cartesian and polar coordinates, where angles are in degrees
+ the scientific method and how it is used
+ the application of chemicals and chemical reactions in engineering
+ the applications of forces and motion in engineering
+ the principles of fluid dynamics and aerodynamics
+ the principles of and the equations used to calculate values in thermodynamic systems.

Exam-style questions

1 An engineering company in the UK is sending an oil tank with a capacity of 2500 litres to a customer in the USA. As such, they need to convert the volume of the tank into gallons. Perform this conversion, giving your answer to the nearest whole number. [2]

2 Convert the Cartesian coordinates (2, 4) into polar coordinates. [3]

3 An engineer has observed that a manufacturing process is producing products with too many defects. Explain how the scientific method could be used to find a solution to this problem. [4]

4 State what a coordinate measuring machine (CMM) is used to measure. [1]

5 Describe two engineering applications of electrolysis. [4]

6 A force of 450N is applied to an area of 2m². Calculate the pressure. [2]

7 Describe the relationship between aerodynamic thrust and drag. [2]

8 A balloon has a volume of 6 litres and is on the ground at sea level, where there is a pressure of 101kPa. The balloon is allowed to climb to an altitude where the pressure is reduced to 50kPa. Assuming a fixed temperature, calculate the final volume of the balloon. [4]

6 Materials and their properties

6.1 Physical and mechanical properties of materials

Physical properties

REVISED

Table 6.1 Physical properties of materials

Property	Description
Density (ϱ)	The mass (m) of material contained per unit volume (V) where $$\rho = \frac{m}{v}$$ Measured in $kg\,m^{-3}$
Melting point	The temperature at which a material changes state from a solid to a liquid
Thermal conductivity (k)	The ability of a material to conduct heat Measured in $W\,m^{-1}\,K^{-1}$
Electrical conductivity (σ)	The ability of a material to conduct electricity Measured in $S\,m^{-1}$
Electrical resistivity (ϱ)	The ability of a material to resist the flow of electricity (resistivity is the inverse of conductivity) Measured in $\Omega\,m$
Coefficient of thermal expansion (α)	The rate at which a material expands or contracts when subject to a change in temperature Measured in $°C^{-1}$
Corrosion resistance	Qualitative indication of the ability of a material to resist the chemical, electrochemical and other processes that cause corrosion
Specific heat capacity (c)	The quantity of heat energy required to raise the temperature of 1 kg of a material by 1 °C Measured in $J\,kg^{-1}\,°C^{-1}$
Hardenability	Qualitative indication of whether heat treatment can alter the crystalline structure of a metal alloy to increase its hardness
Weldability	Qualitative indication of the ability of a material to be welded without cracking or adversely affecting the material's mechanical properties around the joint
Magnetic permeability (μ)	The degree to which a material becomes magnetised in the presence of an external magnetic field; the ratio between the applied magnetic field strength and the magnetic flux density present in the material Measured in $H\,m^{-1}$
Electrical permittivity (ε)	The degree to which a material becomes polarised by an electric field; the ratio between the applied electric field strength and the electric flux density present in the material Measured in $F\,m^{-1}$
Recyclability	Qualitative indication of the degree to which a material is suitable for recycling and subsequent reuse

Density The mass of material per unit volume, represented by the symbol ϱ.

Thermal conductivity The ability of material to conduct heat, represented by the letter k.

Corrosion resistance The ability of a material to resist the processes that cause corrosion.

Recyclability How suitable a material is for recycling.

69

Mechanical properties

Table 6.2 Mechanical properties of materials

Property	Description
Tensile strength (or ultimate tensile stress)	The maximum pulling or tensile stress that a material can withstand before failure
	Measured in $N m^{-1}$ or Pa
Compressive strength (or ultimate compressive stress)	The maximum squeezing or compressive stress that a material can withstand before failure
	Measured in $N m^{-1}$ or Pa
Shear strength (or ultimate shear stress)	The maximum shear stress that a material can withstand before failure
	Measured in $N m^{-1}$ or Pa
Torsional strength (or ultimate torsional stress)	The maximum twisting force or torque that a material can withstand before failure
	Measured in $N m^{-1}$ or Pa
Hardness	How well a material resists surface indentation, scratching or abrasion
	Units of hardness depend on the test methodology used and include the Rockwell hardness number
Toughness	The amount of impact energy a material can absorb up to the point when it fractures
	Measured in $J m^{-3}$
Brittleness	Qualitative description of low toughness in materials that are not impact resistant and shatter easily, or those that undergo little or no plastic elongation before failure when subject to a tensile stress
Ductility	The ability of a material to undergo plastic deformation without failure when subject to a tensile stress
	Can be measured as either the percentage elongation of a test specimen at fracture or percentage reduction in surface area in a test specimen at fracture
Elasticity	Qualitative description of the ability of a deformed material under load to recover its original shape once the load causing the deformation is removed
Plasticity	Qualitative description of the ability of a deformed material under load to retain that deformation permanently when the load is removed
Malleability	The ability of a material to undergo permanent plastic deformation without failure when subject to a compressive stress
	Usually expressed in terms of the compressive strength of the material

Tensile strength The ability of material to resist tensile/pulling stresses.

Compressive strength The ability of material to resist compressive/pushing stresses.

Hardness The ability of material to resist indentations, scratches and abrasions.

Toughness The ability of material to absorb impact energy without fracturing.

Ductility A material's ability to be drawn or stretched without breaking.

Exam tip

Check that you know the differences between physical and mechanical properties and can give examples of both.

Revision activity

Play a mix-and-match game with the names of the material properties shown in the tables above and their definitions. You could do this by writing them out and cutting them into cards to sort.

Now test yourself

TESTED ◯

1 What type of material property is density?
2 What property is a material's ability to withstand scratches and abrasions?
3 What material property is measured in Ωm?

6.2 Types of material and their structures

Types of material

Ferrous metals

+ Ferrous metals are metals that contain iron.
+ Iron is tough, ductile and malleable, but has low tensile strength and relatively low corrosion resistance.
+ In order to increase strength and hardness, iron can be alloyed with carbon to form different grades of carbon steel (low, medium and high).
+ Iron is alloyed with chromium to create stainless steel, which has very high corrosion resistance and is easy to clean. It is, therefore, very useful for kitchen applications and medical equipment.

Non-ferrous metals

+ Non-ferrous metals do not contain iron.
+ They are corrosion resistant and have good thermal and electrical conductivity.
+ Pure examples include aluminium and copper. These metals are used in electrical cables. Nickel and zinc are used in batteries.
+ Examples of alloys are brass and bronze. They are used in plumbing and valve components.
+ Standard forms of supply for metals include plate, sheet, round bar (or rod), square bar, flat bar, round tube, square tube and channel.

Polymers

Thermoplastic polymers

+ Thermoplastic polymers can be moulded into different shapes when heated to a certain temperature.
+ Examples include ABS, HIPS, PLA, polystyrene, polycarbonate, polypropylene and acrylic.
+ These polymers are used in plumbing, packaging and toys.
+ Forms of supply include pellets and sheets.

Thermosetting polymers

+ Thermosetting polymers do not become mouldable when heated. They must be chemically cured in order to be set into the required shapes.
+ Examples include urea formaldehyde, melamine formaldehyde, phenol formaldehyde, epoxy resin and polyester resin. Common applications include plug sockets, pipework and automotive parts.
+ Forms of supply include powders and liquids.

Elastomers

+ Elastomers are flexible polymers consisting of tangled long-chain molecules that are pulled straight into the required shape.
+ Examples include rubber and neoprene, and these are used in the production of tyres and wetsuits.
+ Forms of supply include sheets, rolls and strips.

Composites

+ Composites are materials made up of a combination of distinctly different materials that work together to provide improved mechanical properties.
+ Examples include glass-reinforced polymer (GRP), carbon-reinforced polymer (CRP) and medium-density fibreboard (MDF).
+ Fibre-based composites are usually supplied as separate matrix and reinforcement materials.

> **Alloy** A material that is formed by combining two or more metals.
>
> **Thermoplastic polymers** Polymers that can be moulded into different shapes when heated.
>
> **Thermosetting polymers** Polymers that do not become mouldable when heated.
>
> **Composites** Materials comprising a combination of distinctly different materials that work together to provide improved mechanical properties.

Engineering ceramics

+ Engineering ceramics are inorganic, non-metallic materials with a high melting point.
+ They have high hardness and are good thermal insulators, but are brittle in nature.
+ Examples include silicon carbide (used in abrasives and grinding wheels) and glass.
+ They are often supplied as powders.

Timber

+ Softwoods come from coniferous trees, e.g. pines and firs. They are flexible, light and have relatively low density. They are used as floorboards and shelves.
+ Hardwoods come from deciduous trees, for example oak. They are generally tough and durable, and are used as window frames and doors. However, they can be expensive.
+ Engineered woods are derivative wood products, for example plywood, that are manufactured using timber waste products, such as by combining sawdust, chips or fibres with a resin or adhesive. They are used as flooring and in furniture.
+ Forms of supply include sheets, boards, strips, dowels and shaped mouldings.

Smart materials

+ Smart materials have properties that respond to an external stimulus, for example thermochromic materials change colour when their temperature changes (strip thermometers).
+ Other examples include shape memory alloys (SMAs) used for orthodontic braces, quantum tunnelling composite (QTC) used in pressure sensors, photochromic materials used in sunglasses, and piezoelectric crystals used in microphones.

> **Smart materials** Materials that have properties that respond to an external stimulus, e.g. temperature or light.

Structures

REVISED

Atomic structures

+ Atoms are composed of three types of sub-atomic particle: the nucleus at the centre of an atom contains neutrons and protons, with electrons orbiting the nucleus in a series of orbital layers.
+ Compounds are made up at least two atoms from different elements.

Bonding mechanisms in solids

+ A metallic bond is the force of attraction between free-moving electrons and positive metal ions.
+ Covalent bonds occur when non-metal atoms share a pair of electrons.
+ Ionic bonds occur between a metal and a non-metal, due to the strong electrostatic forces between positively and negatively charged ions.
+ Van der Waals forces are weak intermolecular forces that attract neutral molecules to one another.

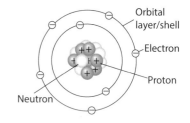

Figure 6.1 Bohr's atomic model of the structure of an atom

> **Metallic bond** The force of attraction between free-moving electrons and positive metal ions.
>
> **Covalent bonds** Bonds that occur when non-metal atoms share a pair of electrons.
>
> **Ionic bonds** Bonds that occur between a metal and a non-metal, due to the strong electrostatic forces between positively and negatively charged ions.

Microstructures and grains in metals

+ When molten metal has cooled to form a solid, small groups of atoms come together and arrange themselves into regular lattice structures. These form numerous seed crystals throughout the material.
+ As the metal cools further, more atoms join each seed crystal and the structures grow and form distinct grains.
+ Individual grains keep growing until they meet other grains that were grown from nearby seed crystals.
+ The orientation of each grain crystal lattice formation differs. Therefore, they do not combine. Instead, they remain separated by grain boundaries.

Lattice structure in metals

+ Solid metals are crystalline, a solid composition of ordered, repeating lattice structures.
+ Dislocations are inconsistencies or gaps in these crystalline lattice structures.
+ Pinning occurs when the movement of dislocation stops. It is caused by the presence of an atom of an alloying element or another dislocation.

Crosslinking of polymers

+ Crosslinking is the process of joining polymer chains together using covalent bonds or short sequences of chemical bonds. They do not form regular crystal lattice structures.
+ Crosslinking can increase mechanical strength.

Ceramic structures

+ A crystalline structure is a structure where the molecules are arranged in an ordered, well-defined crystalline lattice arrangement.
+ An amorphous structure is a non-crystalline structure that does not follow an organised lattice arrangement.
+ Amorphous solids have high hardness but low impact toughness.

Composite structures

+ Composites are made up of a matrix material and a reinforcement material.
+ Particulate composites are comprised of a resin or metal matrix that bonds together particles of the reinforcement material.
+ Fibrous composites are a resin matrix that bonds together fibres of the reinforcement material.
+ Laminated composites use a resin matrix to bond together thin layers or sheets of reinforcement material in a sandwich structure.

Crystalline structure
A structure where the molecules are arranged in an ordered, well-defined lattice arrangement.

Amorphous structure
A non-crystalline structure that does not follow an organised lattice arrangement.

Exam tip

Make sure you know the different types of materials, their properties and common forms of supply.

Revision activity

Create 10 different anagrams using key words associated with materials and their structures. Test these with a partner and discuss their meanings before swapping over roles.

Now test yourself TESTED

4 What type of polymer can be moulded into different shapes when heated to a certain temperature?
5 Name three types of composite material.
6 What is a structure that does not follow an organised arrangement called?
7 What is the cause of pinning in a metal?

6.3 Effects of processing techniques on materials

Processing metals

Forming processes:

+ Rolling is a process whereby metal is passed through two rotating rollers. This shapes the metal into a long, thin layer.
+ Forging is when a material is hammered or pressed into shape once heated.
+ Press forming or moulding is used to shape metal by applying pressure with a press or mould.

Other processing techniques used on metals include the following:

+ Brazing is a joining process whereby a molten filler metal is allowed to flow into the joint, then cools and solidifies.
+ Welding involves localised heating of metal and the introduction of a filler rod to form a molten weld pool. When the weld cools, the material is fused together at the joint.
+ Casting involves pouring molten metal into a prepared mould. The metal is rapidly cooled and solidifies into the desired shape.
+ Sintering is a process in which metal powders are fused using heat and pressure to create a solid object.
+ Coating is the addition of a protective layer to exclude oxygen and prevent damage and corrosion.
+ Hot working involves the plastic deformation of a metal when it is heated above its recrystallisation temperature. When metal is shaped below its recrystallisation temperature it is referred to as cold working.

> **Rolling** A process whereby metal is passed through two rotating rollers, which shapes the metal into a long, thin layer.
>
> **Welding** A joining process which involves heating of a metal and the introduction of a filler rod to form a weld pool that cools and fuses the joint together.
>
> **Casting** A process that involves pouring molten metal into a mould which cools and solidifies into a desired shape.
>
> **Coating** The addition of a protective layer to prevent damage and corrosion.

Effects of processing

Processing polymers

+ In injection moulding a molten thermoplastic is injected into a mould. When this cools and solidifies, the shape is formed. Too high a temperature can cause discolouration and burn marks where trapped air has been compressed and overheated as the mould cavity fills.
+ Thermosetting polymers supplied as powders are compacted into moulds and then heated under pressure to start a chemical curing process. If not given sufficient time to cure, the finished product can have low hardness and low tensile strength.

> **Injection moulding** Molten thermoplastic is injected into a mould, cooled and solidified into a product.

Processing ceramics

+ Sintering for ceramics works in a similar fashion to powder metallurgy.
+ High compaction and high firing temperatures result in high-density and finished products with their optimum mechanical properties.

> **Exam tip**
>
> Ensure you can explain the effects of the different processing techniques on the relevant materials.

Processing composites

+ Fibre-based composites can be manufactured to have anisotropic (direction-dependent) properties by aligning more of the reinforcement fibres in the direction requiring most strength.
+ Areas of additional fibre can also be created to reinforce particular areas of the component around joints and fixings.
+ The tensile strength of fibre-based composite components can be increased by increasing the ratio of reinforcement to resin matrix.

> **Revision activity**
>
> For each material type, produce a mind map of the processing techniques used with them and their effects on the material.

8 Name two joining processes for metals.

9 What type of material is injection moulding used to shape?

10 When processing ceramics, what is the result of high compaction and high firing temperatures?

6.4 Heat treatment and surface treatments

Effects of heat treatments on properties of materials

REVISED ◯

Heat treatments include:

+ case hardening
+ quench hardening
+ tempering
+ normalising
+ annealing
+ precipitation hardening

> **Heat treatment** Processes that use heat in different ways to alter the properties and microstructure of metals.

Surface treatments

REVISED ◯

Surface treatments include:

+ paint applied to the surface of a material to provide a solid, protective film
+ plastic coating to provide metal with a thick protective layer against wear and corrosion
+ galvanising to provide excellent corrosion protection by forming a protective external barrier, preventing steel from oxygen or water damage and providing electrolytic (galvanic) protection.

> **Surface treatment** A process applied to the surface of a material to give it additional wear and corrosion resistance, and/or for aesthetic reasons.

Typical mistake

When asked to explain the effects of processing on materials, do not simply describe the process. This will not give you maximum marks as it is not answering the question that you have been asked. Make sure you read the question properly and answer accordingly.

11 State the purpose of normalising a metal.

12 Name three methods of protecting a material against corrosion.

Revision activity

As available in the workshop, practice using the different processes on the materials stated, and observe how they affect the properties of each material.

6.5 Causes of material failure and their prevention

Corrosion

+ Corrosion is caused by chemical processes that attack and consume a material or degrade its mechanical properties. It can also be caused by exposure to reactive chemicals and material stress.
+ Oxidation occurs when the corroding metal forms an oxide. For example, rust on ferrous metals that are exposed to air and moisture.

> **Corrosion** A chemical process that attacks and consumes a material and degrades its mechanical properties.

Ageing

+ Ageing occurs as a result of gradual degradation processes over a long period of time, for example effects of the weather, exposure to pollutants and other accumulated damage. Ageing is also caused in polymers by exposure to light.

> **Ageing** A process caused by gradual degradation processes over a long time.

Physical causes of material failure

+ Deformation happens when a material changes shape or size. If this occurs beyond its limits it can cause its failure.
+ Fracture occurs when a material separates into two or more parts due to the disconnection of its atomic or molecular bonds.
+ Fatigue causes the failure of materials due to progressive crack growth at stress levels below their yield strength due to cyclic loading.
+ Creep happens when materials are subjected to constant loading well below their yield point but gradually elongate due to plastic deformation and structural degradation. Creep is split into three stages – primary, secondary and tertiary.
+ Erosion is the wearing away of a surface caused by the flow of liquids or gases over it.

> **Fracture** When a material separates into two or more parts due to the disconnection of its atomic or molecular bonds.

Corrosion prevention

+ Corrosion can be prevented by applying coatings, such as plastic coatings or paint, or by galvanisation.
+ Sacrificial anodes are used to 'sacrifice' the more reactive material to protect the main 'cathode' material.

> **Sacrificial anode** A metal that is more likely to corrode than the material that is to be protected.

> **Exam tip**
>
> Make sure you understand the different causes of material failure, including corrosion, aging and physical causes, and how this failure can be prevented.

> **Now test yourself**
>
>
> 13 Give an example of corrosion caused by oxidation.
> 14 Give three causes of ageing in materials.

> **Revision activity**
>
> Research the different ways in which metals corrode. Create a table for each method and add a description of a protection method that could be used to prevent or reduce its effects.

6.6 Materials testing methods and interpretation of results

Methods

REVISED ●

+ Visual inspection is the use of the naked eye to detect defects, without the use of any measuring or testing equipment.
+ Tensile testing measures the response of a material to loading in tension. The material is stretched until it breaks.
+ Toughness can be tested using the Izod test. This involves raising a pivoting arm to a specific height and then releasing it to hit a clamped material. Figure 6.2 shows an Izod impact testing machine.
+ Hardness can be tested through the Brinell, Vickers or Rockwell (HRA, HRB, HRC) tests (see Figure 6.3). All three of these methods involve the indentation of the material.
+ Corrosion resistance testing involves exposing a material to certain conditions of temperature, humidity or other relevant factors and monitoring them for signs of corrosion.
+ Wear resistance is tested using a pin-on disc method, or the use of reciprocating pin. The pins are pressed on to the surface of either a rotating or stationary plate or disc. The wear on the length of the pin and the reduction of thickness of the plate or disc is the overall measure.
+ The Wohler test is used to test fatigue through the use of an S–N curve, where S is the given stress range and N is the number of cycles to failure (see Figure 6.4).
+ Electrical conductivity (σ) of a material can be calculated by first measuring its resistance (R) and then using the formula

$$\sigma \text{ (conductivity)} = \frac{l}{R \times A}$$

where l is the length of the material under test, and A is its cross-sectional area.

Visual inspection The use of the naked eye to detect defects.

Tensile testing Testing that measures the response of a material to loading in tension.

Izod test A method of testing the toughness of a material by raising and releasing a pivoting arm to hit the material.

Wohler test A method of testing fatigue through the use of an S–N curve.

Figure 6.2 Izod impact testing machine

Figure 6.3 Rockwell hardness testing machine

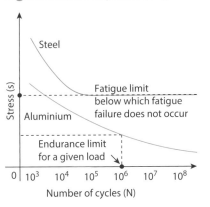

Figure 6.4 S–N curves for typical steel and aluminium alloys

Interpretation of results

+ **Hooke's law** states that, in an elastic material, elongation is directly proportional to load. This is useful when interpreting test data.
+ A load–extension graph can be used to determine several important mechanical properties of a test material, such as its tensile strength, elastic limit, ultimate tensile strength and maximum plastic deformation.
+ **Young's modulus** E is used to calculate how easily a material can stretch and become deformed. Young's modulus can be calculated using the formula

E = stress (σ) / strain (ε)

+ Localised straining or necking leads to a decrease in the cross-sectional area of steel when supporting the test load, and a corresponding increase in localised stress (see Figure 6.7). This increases the rate of localised deformation even further and causes rapid failure.

> **Hooke's law** Law that states that elongation is directly proportional to load.
>
> **Young's modulus (E)** The ratio of tensile stress (σ) to tensile strain (ε).

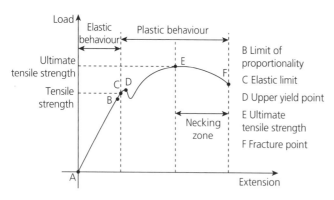

Figure 6.5 Load–extension graph typical of mild steel

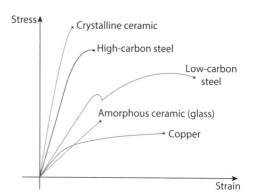

Figure 6.6 Stress–strain characteristics of different materials

---

Now test yourself

15 What is the formula for electrical conductivity?

16 Give **three** tests that can be used to test the hardness of a material.

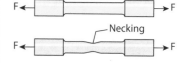

Figure 6.7 Necking formed during the ductile failure of mild steel

---

Summary

In this content area you learned about:

+ the physical and mechanical properties of different materials
+ the different types of materials and their structures
+ the effects of different processing techniques on materials
+ the effects of heat treatments and surface treatments on materials
+ the causes of material failure and prevention methods
+ how materials are tested and how the results are interpreted.

Exam tip

Make sure that you can calculate Young's modulus, the test of stress and strain. Always show all of your working in your responses.

Exam-style questions

1 Explain the difference between tensile and compressive strength. [2]

2 State what is meant by the hardness of material. [1]

3 Describe the properties of iron. [4]

4 Explain the difference between a crystalline and an amorphous structure. [2]

5 Describe the effects of too high temperature when injection moulding polymers. [3]

6 Explain the effects of annealing on a material. [3]

7 Explain, using an example, how material ageing occurs. [3]

8 Give the three stages of creep. [3]

9 Explain how necking results in the failure of steel. [4]

Revision activity

Use a range of tests to test the properties of different materials. List the steps you took and the outcome of each test. You could present your results as a table.

Check your understanding and progress at **www.hoddereducation.co.uk/myrevisionnotes**

7 Mechanical principles

7.1 Principles of motion and mechanics in engineering and manufacturing systems

Newton's three laws of motion

+ Newton's first law of motion states that a body will remain at rest, or will continue moving at a constant speed in a straight line, unless a force is acting upon it.
+ Newton's second law of motion states that the acceleration of an object depends on the mass of the object itself and the net force acting upon it. This is represented by the formula

Force (F) = mass (m) × acceleration (a)

+ Newton's third law of motion states that for every action or force, there is an equal and opposite reaction. For example, gravity where the Earth exerts force of attraction on an object and in turn the object exerts force in the opposite direction.

> **Newton's laws of motion** Three laws that describe the relationship between the motion of objects and the forces acting on them.

Types of forces

Table 7.1 Types of forces

Type of force	Explanation
Concurrent forces (see Figure 7.1)	Where the lines of action all meet at the same point, e.g. the forces on the bob of a swinging pendulum
Non-concurrent forces	e.g. a ladder resting against a wall
Co-planar forces	Forces that are all acting in the same plane, e.g. tug of war
Non-contact forces	Forces that act between objects that do not physically touch each other, e.g. magnets
Reaction forces	Forces that act in opposition to an action force in line with Newton's third law of motion, e.g. friction
Shear forces (see Figure 7.2)	Forces that act in a parallel direction to the surface of an object, e.g. a knife cutting through an object

> **Concurrent forces** Forces where the lines of action all meet at the same point.
>
> **Co-planar forces** Forces that are all acting in the same plane.

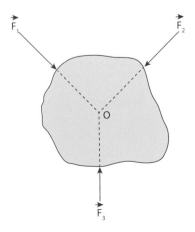

Figure 7.1 Concurrent forces

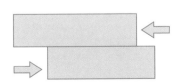

Figure 7.2 The potential effects of shear forces on a component

79

Simply supported beams and loads

+ Beams are long structural elements that are designed to withstand various different loads.
+ Simply supported beams are beams that are resting on two supports, and that are free to move horizontally.
+ Loads are the forces acting on a beam, for example the weight of cars on a bridge.
+ A point load is a force applied at a single point on a beam.
+ A uniformly distributed load is applied evenly over the entire area or length of a beam.
+ Some loads can be a combination of point and uniformly distributed loads.
+ Bending moments are a measure of the bending effect that occurs when a force is applied to a beam or other structural component.

Simply supported beams
Beams that are resting on two supports and free to move horizontally.

Point load A load that is applied at a single point on a beam.

Uniformly distributed load A load that is applied evenly over the entire area or length of a beam.

Now test yourself
TESTED

1 What does Newton's first law of motion state?

2 State the mathematical representation of Newton's second law of motion.

3 What type of load is applied evenly over the entire area or length of a beam?

4 What is a bending moment?

Revision activity

Set up a test rig for a simply supported beam. Apply different loads and note the response of the beam.

Exam tip

Ensure you know the differences between Newton's three laws of motion and how they are applied.

7.2 Principles of forces and energy

Forces and energy

Conservation of momentum and energy

+ It is not possible for either momentum or energy to be created or destroyed.
+ The total momentum of two or more objects acting on each other remains constant unless an external force is applied, and is represented mathematically as

$$m_1 u_1 + m_2 u_2 = m_1 v_1 + m_2 v_2$$

where m_1 and m_2 are masses of the objects, u_1 and u_2 are the initial velocities of the objects, and v_1 and v_2 are the final velocities of the objects.

+ Energy can only be changed from one form to another. This is represented mathematically as

$$K_1 + U_1 = K_2 + U_2$$

where K_1 is the initial kinetic energy, U_1 is the initial potential energy, K_2 is the final kinetic energy and U_2 is the final potential energy.

Table 7.2 Forces and energy

Name of force or energy	Definition
D'Alembert's principle	An alternative way of expressing Newton's second law of motion
	It states that the force plus the negative of the mass multiplied by the acceleration is equal to zero, that is, $F - ma = 0$
Potential and kinetic energy	Potential energy is the energy that is stored by an object due to its position
	Kinetic energy is the energy that an object possesses because it is moving
	When potential energy is released, it is changed into kinetic energy
Gravitational force	The force that attracts all objects with mass towards each other
	The Earth exerts a gravitational force that attracts objects towards its centre
	At the surface of the Earth, the acceleration due to gravity is approximately 9.81 m/s^2
Frictional resistance (see Figure 7.3)	**Friction** is a force that acts in opposition to an object moving along a surface, e.g. where a cutting tool meets the workpiece when machining
	Friction (F) = Coefficient of friction (μ) × normal force (N)
	Often generates heat, which can cause the failure of tools, components and equipment
Mechanical work	The amount of energy that is transferred by a force acting on an object
	Measured in joules (J)
	Work (W) = Force (F) × distance moved by object (d)
Power	The rate at which energy is transferred or converted
	$\text{Power}\,(P) = \dfrac{\text{work done}\,(E)}{\text{time taken}\,(t)}$

D'Alembert's principle States that the force plus the negative of the mass multiplied by the acceleration is equal to zero, that is, $F - ma = 0$.

Potential energy Energy that is stored by an object due to its position.

Kinetic energy Energy that an object possesses because of its motion.

Gravitational force Force that attracts all objects with mass towards each other.

Friction Force that acts in opposition to an object moving along a surface.

Mechanical work The amount of energy that is transferred by a force.

Power The rate at which energy is transferred or converted.

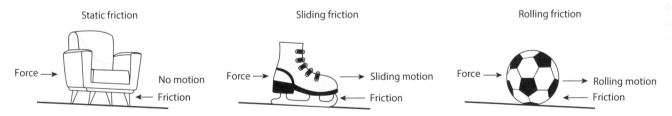

Figure 7.3 Different types of friction

Types of power sources

+ Mechanical power sources create energy through mechanical motion, such as vibrations or pressure.
+ Electrical power sources generate energy in the form of electricity.
+ Renewable power sources come from resources that are naturally replenished and sustainable. Examples are given in Table 7.3.

> **Renewable power sources** Power sources that come from resources that are naturally replenished and sustainable.

Table 7.3 Power sources

Power source	Function	Advantages
Solar	Solar panels (see Figure 7.4) create a current when sunlight strikes them, because of the ejection of electrons from the silicon material	Renewable and sustainable source of power Zero carbon emissions Clean source of power Produces a lot of electricity in sunny environments
Hydro	Water is slowly released from behind a dam to turn turbines. These then turn generators to produce electricity	Renewable and sustainable source of power Low carbon emissions Clean source of power Can produce large quantities of power
Wind	Turbines are turned by the power of the wind (see Figure 7.4). These then turn generators to produce electricity	Renewable and sustainable source of power Low carbon emissions Clean source of power Produces a lot of electricity in windy environments, such as on top of hills
Biofuels	Fuels are made from biomass, which is produced using plant and animal waste. These can then be used to replace fossil fuels in power-generation applications	Renewable and sustainable source of power Reduced carbon emissions Reduces reliance on fossil fuels
Geothermal	Steam created from hot water below the surface of the Earth is used to turn turbines. These then turn generators to produce electricity	Renewable and sustainable source of power Clean and quiet Has relatively little impact on the environment compared to the use of fossil fuels
Electric motors/generators	Electric motors use the principle of electromagnetism to produce rotary movement when an electric current is applied Electric generators work in reverse to motors in order to produce electricity from rotary movement	Generators are a key component of most power-generation systems, e.g. fossil-fuel power stations, wind turbines and hydro systems Relatively cheap and widely understood technology
Internal combustion	Heat energy from burning fuel (such as petrol or diesel) is converted into movement Internal combustion engines consist of fixed cylinders and moving pistons	Relatively small and portable Relatively simple to maintain Relatively cheap and widely understood technology
Fossil fuels	Coal, oil and gas are burned to create steam that turns turbines. These then turn generators to produce electricity	Still readily available Relatively cheap source of energy Can be used to generate large quantities of power
Nuclear	Nuclear fission creates steam which is used to turn turbines. These then turn generators to produce electricity	Reduced carbon emissions Can be used to generate large quantities of power Reduces reliance on fossil fuels

Figure 7.4 Solar panels and wind turbines

> **Typical mistake**
>
> Different power sources allow electricity to be produced in different ways. Make sure you do not confuse them.

> **Exam tip**
>
> Make sure you know and can use the correct formulae to calculate values for power and work done.

Now test yourself TESTED ○

5 What is the value of gravity at the Earth's surface?

6 What is the formula for mechanical work?

7 Name two examples of renewable power sources.

8 What power source makes use of a fission reaction to create steam for turning turbines?

> **Revision activity**
>
> With a partner, discuss the relative advantages of using different types of power sources to create electricity.

Summary

In this content area you learned about:
+ Newton's three laws of motion
+ the different types of forces that can act on objects
+ what is meant by a simply supported beam and the different types of load that act on them
+ the principles of the conservation of momentum and energy
+ the different types of power sources and their relative advantages and disadvantages.

Exam-style questions

1 State Newton's third law of motion. [1]

2 A motor vehicle has a mass of 1500 kg. Calculate the engine force needed to produce an acceleration of 2.5 m/s². [2]

3 A machine tool is suffering from excessive friction with a workpiece. Explain how this could affect the condition of the tool. [2]

4 Explain the difference between a point load and a uniformly distributed load on a beam. [2]

5 A box of materials is pushed with a force of 200 N for a distance of 15 m. Calculate the work done to the box. [2]

6 The work done to move a crate is 50 J and the time taken to do this is 20 seconds. Calculate the power needed to move the crate. [2]

7 Explain two advantages of wind power. [4]

8 Describe how fossil fuels are used to produce power. [3]

9 Explain one advantage and one disadvantage of nuclear power. [4]

8 Electrical and electronic principles

8.1 Principles of electrical and electronic systems

Basic principles of electricity and electronics

Charge, current and electron flow

+ Electrical charge is either positive or negative.
+ Electrons are negatively charged particles.
+ Protons are positively charged particles.
+ Conventional current is a flow of protons – positive to negative.
+ In reality, current is a flow of electrons – negative to positive.
+ Current is measured in amperes or 'amps' (A).
+ Resistance is the opposition to the flow of current, measured in ohms (Ω).
+ Conductors are materials that allow current to flow through them, whereas resistors restrict the flow of current.

Electrical energy, power and force

Table 8.1 SI units of measurement for the main electrical parameters

Parameter	Unit of measurement	Unit abbreviation
Voltage	volt	V
Current	ampere (amp)	A
Resistance	ohm	Ω
Power	watt	W
Capacitance	farad	F
Inductance	henry	H
Energy	joule	J
Time	seconds	s
Frequency	hertz	Hz
Magnetic flux	weber	Wb
Magnetic flux density	tesla	T

Electrons Negatively charged particles.

Current A flow of electrons, measured in amps (A). Can be direct (DC) or alternating (AC).

Resistance The opposition to the flow of current, measured in ohms (Ω).

Electrical energy The capacity for an electrical circuit to do work.

Electrical power The rate at which electrical energy is transferred.

Electrical force The attractive or repulsive interaction between two charged objects.

Table 8.2 Electricity information

Term	Meaning	Unit of measurement
Electrical energy	The capacity for an electrical circuit to do work. Energy E = power P × time t	joules (J)
Electrical power	The rate at which electrical energy is transferred. Power P = current I × voltage V Power P = current I^2 × resistance R	watts (W)
Electrical force	The attractive or repulsive interaction between two charged objects	newtons (N)

Check your understanding and progress at **www.hoddereducation.co.uk/myrevisionnotes**

Networks and elements

+ An electrical network is an arrangement of connected electrical or electronic components.
+ Electrical elements are idealised representations of the actual electrical components in a network. For example, resistors, capacitors and inductors.

Capacitance

+ Capacitance is the ability of a component to store charge.
+ It is measured in farads (F).

Magnetism

+ A magnetic field is the area surrounding a magnet where magnetic forces are observable.
+ The field strength is the intensity of the magnetic field.
+ Magnetic flux is the total magnetic field that passes through a given area.
+ Magnetic flux density is the amount of magnetic flux that passes through a given area at right angles to the magnetic field.

Electromagnetism

+ Electromagnetic induction occurs when a magnet moves within a coil of wire, producing a voltage.
+ Applications of electromagnetism include electric generators, transformers, computer hard disks (drives) and maglev trains (a levitating, high-speed train that takes advantage of a lack of friction).

Figure 8.1 A maglev train

Measurements of electrical quantities

+ The most common piece of equipment used to measure electrical quantities is a multimeter.
+ This can measure voltage (volts), current (amps) and resistance (ohms).
+ Some multimeters can also check for continuity in a circuit.

Figure 8.2 A digital multimeter

Electric circuit theories

REVISED ○

Voltage

+ The difference in the electric potential between two points in a circuit.
+ Also known as potential difference.
+ Measured in volts (V).

> **Electrical network** An arrangement of connected electrical or electronic components.
>
> **Capacitance** The ability of a component to store charge, measured in farads (F).
>
> **Magnetic flux density** The amount of magnetic flux that passes through a given area at right angles to the magnetic field.
>
> **Electromagnetic induction** The production of a voltage when a magnet moves within a coil of wire.

> **(Voltage) potential difference** The difference in the electric potential between two points in a circuit, measured in volts (V).

Types of current

+ Current is the flow of electrons through a circuit.
+ Alternating current (AC) changes direction periodically.
+ Direct current (DC) flows in one direction only.

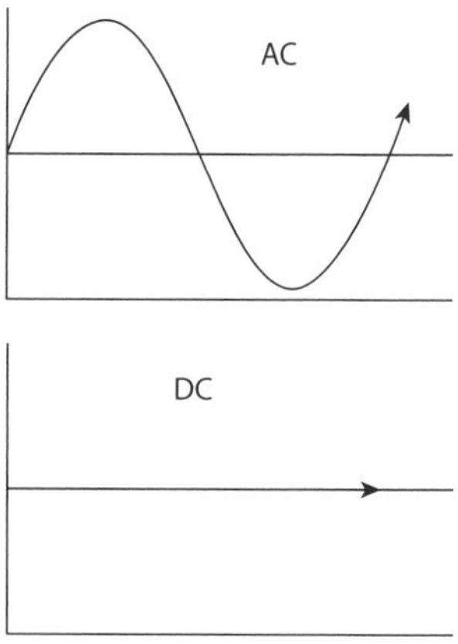

Potential dividers

+ A potential divider is a circuit that uses resistors to divide the initial supply voltage, resulting in a smaller output voltage.
+ The output voltage is calculated using the formula

$$V_o = \frac{R_2}{(R_1 + R_2)} \times V_s$$

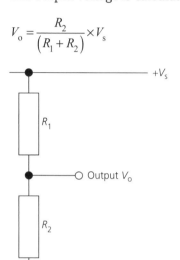

Figure 8.4 A potential divider circuit

Ohm's law

+ Ohm's law gives the relationship between voltage V, current I and resistance R.
+ Expressed as $V = I \times R$.

Series, parallel and combination circuits

+ In series circuits components are connected in a line and there is only one path for current to flow through.
+ In parallel circuits the components are connected in branches or loops, and there are at least two paths that the current can flow through.
+ Combination circuits have some components connected in series and some connected in parallel.
+ The total resistance of resistors connected in series is calculated using the formula: $R_{tot} = R_1 + R_2 + R_3 + \ldots$
+ The total resistance of resistors connected in parallel is calculated using the formula: $\frac{1}{R_{tot}} = \frac{1}{R_1} + \frac{1}{R_2} + \frac{1}{R_3} + \ldots$

Kirchhoff's current and voltage laws

+ Kirchhoff's current law states that the total current or charge entering a node is equal to the charge leaving the node.
+ Kirchhoff's voltage law states that in any closed-loop network, the total voltage around the loop is equal to the sum of all the voltage drops within the loop.
+ Kirchoff's laws are applied when it is not possible to use Ohm's law to model the behaviour of more complex circuits.

Figure 8.3 AC and DC transmissions

> **Ohm's law** A law that gives the relationship between voltage, current and resistance.

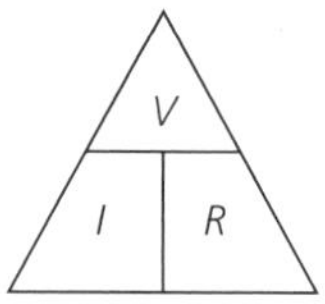

Figure 8.5 Ohm's law triangle

> **Series circuit** A circuit arrangement where components are connected in a line.
>
> **Parallel circuit** A circuit arrangement where the components are connected in branches or loops.

Check your understanding and progress at **www.hoddereducation.co.uk/myrevisionnotes**

Phasor diagrams

In AC circuits, phasor diagrams show the phase relationships between two or more alternating quantities (sine waves with the same frequency) in terms of their magnitude and direction.

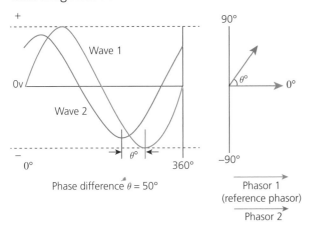

Phase difference $\theta = 50°$

Figure 8.6 Waveform diagram and phasor diagram

> **Phasor diagram** A diagram that shows the phase relationships between two or more alternating quantities in terms of their magnitude and direction.
>
> **Circuit protection systems** Safety systems that protect circuits from damage in the event of unusual conditions, such as too much voltage or current.

Circuit protection systems

Table 8.3 describes some circuit protection systems.

Table 8.3 Circuit protection systems

Circuit protection system	What it does
Time graded over current protection	Incorporates the use of time discrimination to ensure that the circuit breaker nearest the fault opens first
Lightning arrestor	Uses high-voltage and ground terminals to divert the current from a lightning strike to earth
Distance protection system	Measures the opposition to the AC current between a relay and a fault location, and compares this measurement with a set value. If the measured value is less than this set value, the relay isolates the fault
Residual current device (RCDs)	Cuts off the power supply ('trips') if there is an imbalance between the neutral and live wires in an electrical circuit
Differential protection system	Checks that that the current flowing into a transmission line also comes out of it

DC circuit networks

REVISED

+ DC networks are arrangements of components that use low-voltage and direct current power supplies.
+ Resistors are components that reduce the flow of current. The greater the resistance of the resistor, the less current can flow through it.
+ Capacitors temporarily store charge in an electric field between two metal plates.
+ Inductors use a coil of wire to store energy in the form of a magnetic field.
+ Resistors, capacitors and inductors can all be arranged in series, parallel and combined circuits.

Semiconductors

+ Semiconductors are materials that conduct current more efficiently than insulators, but not as well as conductors.
+ N-type semiconductors have electrons as the majority charge carriers.
+ P-type semiconductors have electron holes as the majority charge carriers.

> **Inductors** Components that use a coil of wire to store energy in the form of a magnetic field.
>
> **N-type semiconductors** Semiconductors that have electrons as the majority charge carriers.
>
> **P-type semiconductors** Semiconductors that have holes as the majority charge carriers.

+ When P- and N-type semiconductors are combined, this forms a P-N junction.
+ Forward bias is when current flows through a P-N junction from positive to negative when a positive voltage is applied to the P-type side of the junction. Current cannot flow in the opposite direction.
+ Reverse bias occurs when a positive voltage is applied to the N-type side of the junction. No current flows until the electric field intensity is so high that the junction breaks down.
+ The most common application of forward and reverse bias is in diodes.
+ Transistors (a semiconductor device that can control or regulate electrical signal flow) consist of two P-N junctions, i.e. NPN or PNP.

Hierarchical design

+ A way of designing circuits where parts and components are divided into different blocks and sub-blocks, grouped according to their function.
+ New blocks can be created for new components and old blocks can be reused as necessary. This saves time and increases efficiency.

Signals

+ Analogue signals are continuous and can take any value within a given range. They are measured in sinusoidal waves.
+ Digital signals are discrete, shown as either 1 (high) or 0 (low). They are measured in square waves.
+ Both types of signals can be represented as waveforms and are shown as a graph of voltage against time.
+ The different types of signal waveforms include: sinusoidal, square, rectangular, triangular and sawtooth (Figure 8.7), named because of their shapes.
+ An oscilloscope can be used to measure the characteristics of electrical signal waveforms.
+ Signal processing is when a signal is synthesised, modified and/or analysed in some way, e.g. filtering out noise from an audio signal.
+ Signal conditioning is when signals are manipulated and prepared for the next stage of processing.

Analogue signals Continuous signals that can take any value within a given range.

Digital signals Discrete signals that are either 1 (high) or 0 (low).

Exam tip

Ensure all answers to calculations are given in the correct units. There will sometimes be marks allocated for this.

Exam tip

Use the $V = IR$ triangle to help you when calculating values using Ohm's law.

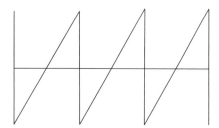

Figure 8.7 Sawtooth wave

Fan in and fan out

+ Fan in is the number of inputs that a logic gate is capable of dealing with safely. A logic gate outputs digital signals that depend on the value of the input signals.
+ Fan out is the number of logic gate inputs that are driven by the output of another logic gate.

Typical mistake

When calculating electrical quantities, learners often miss out steps of the calculation. Make sure you include all the working in your calculations.

Now test yourself

1 What is the attractive or repulsive interaction between two charged objects?

2 What quantity is calculated using the formula, $E = P \times t$?

3 What is calculated using the formula

$$V_o = \frac{R_2}{(R_1 + R_2)} \times V_s ?$$

4 What electrical quantity is measured in farads?

5 What is voltage also known as?

6 What is the formula for adding resistors in series?

7 Which law states that in any closed-loop network, the total voltage around the loop is equal to the sum of all the voltage drops within the loop.

8 Which type of signal is shown as either 1 (high) or 0 (low)?

9 What is filtering out noise from an audio signal an example of?

10 State what is meant by fan in, in relation to logic systems?

Revision activity

Produce a short presentation about how different circuit protection methods work. Present this to the class, your tutor or a partner.

Revision activity

Place two magnets under a piece of paper, firstly with attractive poles facing each other and then with repulsive poles facing each other. For each layout, sprinkle iron filings over the paper and the two magnets. What does this show you about how magnetic fields work?

Revision activity

Use CAD software to simulate how resistors, capacitors and inductors function. Produce annotated screenshots explaining your findings.

Summary

In this content area you learned about:

+ the basic definitions and principles that underpin electrical and electronic systems and devices
+ the relationship between magnetic flux density and field strength
+ the difference between series, parallel and combinational circuits
+ the application of Ohm's law and other circuit theories to calculate values in circuits
+ how different circuit protection methods work
+ the characteristics of different signals and signal types, and the types of waveforms used
+ the components used in DC networks
+ the properties and applications of semiconductor materials and components, including forward and reverse bias
+ what is meant by fan in and fan out in logic circuits.

Exam-style questions

1 Define conventional current flow. [1]

2 Explain the relationship between magnetic flux density and field strength. [3]

3 Two 12 Ω resistors are connected together in a series arrangement. The current flowing through the arrangement is 1.5 A. Calculate the voltage across the resistor arrangement. [3]

4 Two 10 Ω resistors are connected in parallel. Calculate the total resistance. [3]

5 Explain the purpose of Kirchoff's laws. [2]

6 Give three applications of electromagnetic induction. [3]

7 An engineer is designing a new electricity pylon. The pylon will be placed in an open field and will be 36 m tall. Explain why they should include a lightning arrestor on the pylon design. [3]

8 Explain the differences between forward and reverse bias in relation to the properties of P-N junctions. [4]

9 Mechatronics

9.1 The key components of a mechatronics system

Mechatronics is the integration of mechanical and electronic systems to produce a functioning system, e.g. robot arms used to assemble products or perform maintenance, or smartphones with accelerometers to detect movement.

Mechanical components

Table 9.1 Mechanical components

Component	Purpose and function	Visual of component
Gears	Toothed wheels that are linked together to transmit drive Two or more gears linked together are called a gear train Gear ratio $= \dfrac{\text{number of teeth on driven gear}}{\text{number of teeth on driver gear}}$	 **Figure 9.1** A simple gear train
Cams	Mechanisms that work with a follower (the part that rises and falls) to turn rotary motion into linear or reciprocating motion The follower is rotated, either manually or by using a motor, causing the follower to move up and down	 **Figure 9.2** A cam and follower mechanism

> **Gear** A toothed wheel that is linked together with others to transmit drive.

Component	Purpose and function	Visual of component
Linkages	Systems made up of levers or rods connected together via fixed or moveable pivots Used to change the size of a force and/or the direction or type of motion depending on the type, e.g. reverse motion, parallel motion and bell cranks	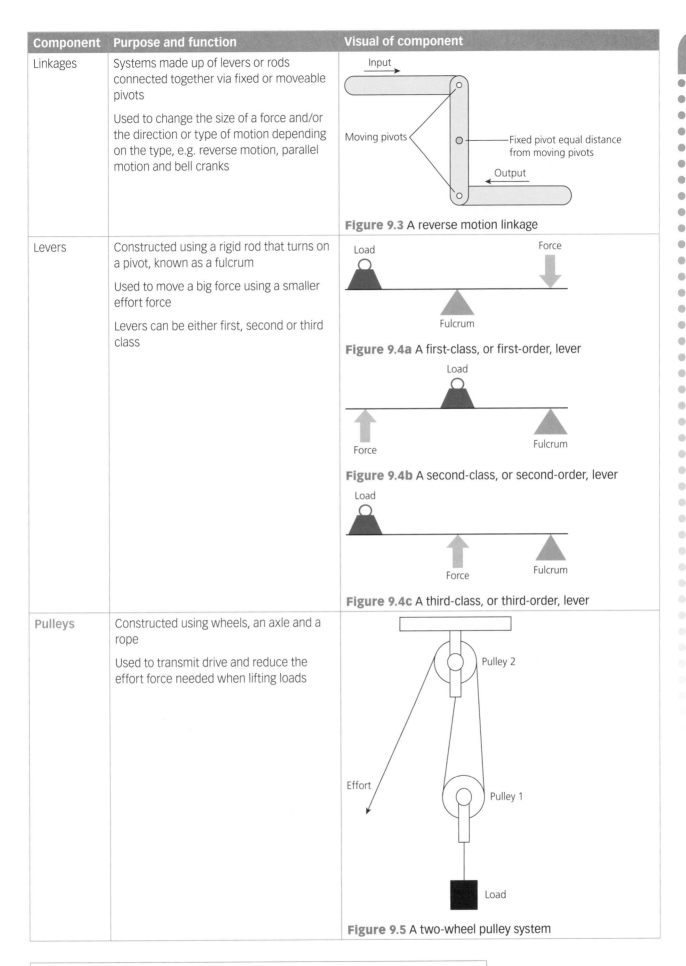 **Figure 9.3** A reverse motion linkage
Levers	Constructed using a rigid rod that turns on a pivot, known as a fulcrum Used to move a big force using a smaller effort force Levers can be either first, second or third class	**Figure 9.4a** A first-class, or first-order, lever **Figure 9.4b** A second-class, or second-order, lever **Figure 9.4c** A third-class, or third-order, lever
Pulleys	Constructed using wheels, an axle and a rope Used to transmit drive and reduce the effort force needed when lifting loads	**Figure 9.5** A two-wheel pulley system

Pulley A mechanism made using wheels, an axle and a rope, that enables loads to be lifted with less effort.

91

Electrical/electronic components

Table 9.2 Electrical/electronic components

Component	Purpose and function
Sensors	Convert signals from the physical environment into an electrical or electronic signal (e.g. voltage, current or resistance)
	Used to detect changes in the environment, for example, changes in light, sound or temperature levels
Transducers	Electrical/electronic sensors (input devices) and actuators (output devices)
	Convert one form of energy, or signal, into another
Microprocessors	Use a central processing unit (CPU) on a programmable integrated circuit (IC) to control devices
	Mainly used in computer-based systems, e.g. computer-controlled robots
Microcontrollers	Acts as a small computer on a chip
	Is programmed to perform different functions, such as responding to sensors and actuating outputs
Actuators	Convert electrical, electronic or mechanical signals into physical movement
	Common examples are motors (rotary motion) and solenoids (pushing or pulling motion)

> **Sensor** A component that converts signals from the physical environment into an electrical or electronic signal.
>
> **Microcontroller** A small computer on a chip that is programmed to perform different functions.
>
> **Actuator** A device that converts electrical, electronic or mechanical signals into physical movement.

Common drive devices

Table 9.3 Common drive devices

Component	Purpose and function
Standard **motor**	Creates rotary motion when current flows through it
	Varying the supply voltage varies the speed of rotation
Servo motor	Creates rotary motion through a precise angle or velocity
	The movement of the motor is controlled by a series of electronic pulses
Stepper motor	Creates rotary motion through a series of precise steps
	Each full 360-degree rotation is divided into a sequence of equal steps

> **Motor** A device that creates rotary motion when current flows through it.

1 What mechanical device is constructed from levers or rods connected together via pivots?
2 State the function of an actuator.
3 Name two examples of programmable components.
4 What type of component creates rotary motion through a series of precise steps?

Exam tip

Make sure you know the differences between the different types of motors and how they work.

Revision activity

Produce a presentation about different mechanical and electrical/electronic components: how they work and why they are used. Create visual aids and present your findings to your class, tutor or another student.

9.2 The operation, function and applications of programmable logic controllers in mechatronic systems

Programmable logic controllers (PLCs) are used in industrial control systems to control different production processes. They are programmable devices that are rugged and reliable, so ideal for use in manufacturing environments.

> **Programmable logic controller (PLC)** A programmable device used to control manufacturing and production processes.

Types of PLCs

+ Unitary PLCs have all the different parts and components contained within a single housing.
+ Modular PLCs have different parts, or modules, all connected together to form a customisable device.
+ Some PLCs contain both unitary and modular features.

> **Unitary PLCs** PLCs that have all the different parts and components contained within a single housing.
>
> **Modular PLCs** PLCs that have different parts, or modules, that are connected together to form a customisable device.

PLC architecture

PLCs consist of a power supply, a central processing unit (CPU), a programming device and ports for connecting the input and output devices.

Operation of PLCs

+ PLCs must be programmed using an appropriate language or system. An example is ladder logic. This presents instructions as a graphical diagram based on relay logic hardware.
+ Signal conditioning is the modification of a signal from a sensor or other device so that it can be processed by a PLC. For example, converting analogue signals to digital signals, or filtering unwanted noise from a signal.

PLC function

+ PLCs are represented as process blocks within systems block diagrams.
+ Motor drivers are used when a PLC cannot provide the required output current to drive one or more motors on its own. For example, the L293D IC, which can drive motors both forwards and backwards.
+ Interface devices ensure accurate communication takes place between a PLC and its input and output devices.

> **Motor driver** An integrated circuit (IC) that is used to ensure that the motors have the correct current to function.

Applications of PLCs

Examples of applications of PLCs in manufacturing and control include:
+ robotic arms on production and assembly lines
+ conveyor belt control systems
+ automated packaging systems
+ animatronic systems, e.g. hands and arms
+ remote technical units.

Supervisory control and data acquisition (SCADA) software is used to monitor and control industrial engineering processes. A SCADA system typically consists of a PLC, supervisory computers, remote terminal units, communications devices and a human-machine interface (HMI).

> **Supervisory control and data acquisition (SCADA)** A PLC-based system that is used to monitor and control industrial engineering processes.

Now test yourself TESTED

Now test yourself — TESTED

5 What does PLC stand for?

6 What type of PLC has different parts that are connected together to form a customisable device?

7 What is the purpose of a SCADA system?

Typical mistake

It is easy to confuse the different types of PLCs. Make sure you understand the differences between unitary PLCs, modular PLCs and PLCs with both unitary and modular features.

Revision activity

Design and program a PLC-based system to control a conveyor belt on a production line. Explain how your system works, and its advantages and limitations.

9.3 The basic principles of hydraulics and pneumatics

Hydraulic and pneumatic systems use fluid power as the power and signal transmission medium.

✚ Hydraulic systems use a liquid, such as oil or water. They can provide high amounts of power, but can lack speed compared to pneumatic systems.

✚ Pneumatic systems use compressed air. They can provide high control speed, but can lack power compared to hydraulic systems.

Fluid power systems can be represented as schematic diagrams by drawing the different components as symbols and linking them together.

Table 9.4 Fluid power system components

Component	Type of fluid power system(s) typically used in	Purpose and function
Valve	Hydraulic and pneumatic	Controls the direction of the fluid and hence the movement of other components
		Arranged in different layouts to create AND and OR systems
Pump	Hydraulic	Creates the flow of fluid by overcoming the pressure induced by the resistive load
Actuator	Hydraulic and pneumatic	Turns the hydraulic or pneumatic energy back into mechanical energy
		Acts as an output device to the system
Cylinder	Hydraulic and pneumatic	An example of an actuator within a fluid power system
		Forces a piston to move in a certain direction
		The movement is created by a rod moving backwards and forwards within a barrel
Compressor	Pneumatic	Converts electrical or mechanical energy into pressurised air

Hydraulic system A fluid power system that uses a liquid as the power transmission medium.

Pneumatic system A fluid power system that uses compressed air as the power transmission medium.

Fluid power components The different parts that are connected together to form a fluid power system.

Exam tip

Check that you understand the purpose and function of the components used in fluid power systems.

Revision activity

Use CAD software to simulate the function of the different component used in fluid power systems. Annotate your simulations to explain how each component works.

Now test yourself — TESTED

8 Which fluid power system uses compressed air as the power medium?

9 What type of fluid power system is typically used where greater power is required?

10 Describe the function of a valve in a fluid power system.

Summary

In this content area you learned about:
+ the purpose and function of mechanical components, electrical/electronic components and common drive devices
+ the different types of PLCs
+ how PLCs operate and function
+ the applications of PLCs in engineering and manufacturing
+ the differences between hydraulic and pneumatic systems
+ the components used in hydraulic and pneumatic systems.

Exam-style questions

1 Name three types of lever. [3]

2 A two-gear train has a driver gear with 60 teeth and a driven gear of 20 teeth. Calculate the gear ratio of this gear train. [2]

3 Explain the purpose of a pulley system. [2]

4 Describe how a servo motor functions. [2]

5 An engineer is designing an automated climate control system for a motor vehicle. The system must be able to keep the temperature at the level set by the driver. Identify a suitable input sensor for the system and describe how it would function. [4]

6 Give four applications of PLCs in manufacturing. [4]

7 Explain the difference between unitary and modular PLCs. [2]

8 Describe the purpose of a hydraulic actuator. [2]

10 Engineering and manufacturing and control systems

10.1 Principles and applications of control system theory

Control and instrumentation systems are used to monitor and control manufacturing and production processes. They achieve this through the use of input sensors, process devices and outputs.

Input devices

Inputs take a signal from the environment and turn it into a signal that can be understood by a process device, for example, a digital voltage signal. Examples of input devices include light, temperature, flow and pressure sensors.

Process devices

Process devices are the 'brains' of a control system. They respond to input signals and alter them in some way, before sending them to the output blocks to be actuated.

Table 10.1 Examples of process devices

Process device	Description
Logic gates	A type of process device that responds to and produces digital signals (1s and 0s). Types include AND, OR and NOT gates. AND gates produce an output signal of 1 when both input signals are 1. OR gates produce an output signal of 1 when either of the input signals are 1. NOT gates produce an output signal that is the opposite of the input signal.
Timers	Produce a signal that stays high or low for a set period of time
Comparators	Compare two different signals and indicate which is the highest
Pulse units	Produce a continuous sequence of digital pulses
Counters	Add up the number of digital signals or pulses received
Latches	Produce a signal that stays high or low until reset

Output devices

Output devices take the signal from a process device and turn it back into an environmental signal, such as light, sound or movement. Examples of output devices include light-emitting diodes (that produce light), buzzers (that produce sound) and actuators (that produce movement).

Electrical signal   Real-world signal

Figure 10.1 An output block in an electrical control system

Signals

Signals can be either analogue or digital. Analogue signals are shown as waveforms that can have continually changing values, for example sinusoidal waves (see Figure 10.2). Digital signals are discrete signals that can only be high (1) or low (0). They are shown as square waves (see Figure 10.3).

Input A device that takes a signal from the environment and turns it into a signal that can be understood by a process device.

Process A device that responds to input signals and alters them in some way.

Output A device that takes the signal from a process device and turns it back into an environmental signal.

Exam tip

Make sure you can both interpret and draw different representations of control and instrumentation systems.

Revision activity

Use CAD software to test the function of different input, process and output components. Use annotated screenshots to explain how they work.

Check your understanding and progress at **www.hoddereducation.co.uk/myrevisionnotes**

Figure 10.2 An analogue signal

Figure 10.3 A digital signal

Open- and closed-loop systems

Closed-loop systems have one or more feedback loops, whereas open-loop systems do not. In a feedback loop, the output signal from a system becomes an input signal to the same system. For example, heating systems in homes are controlled by thermostats in closed-loop systems. The thermostat switches the heating on when the temperature in the room drops below the desired or set temperature.

An advantage of closed-loop systems is that they are less likely to be affected by noise. This means that they are more reliable and accurate. The disadvantage of closed-loop systems is that they are costly to produce and maintain. A system whose behaviour depends on explicit values of time is called a time dependent system.

Underdamped systems oscillate through the equilibrium position. Overdamped systems move more slowly towards this position.

Figure 10.4 An open-loop system

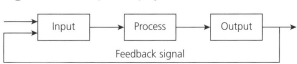

Figure 10.5 A closed-loop system

> **Feedback** When the output signal from a system becomes an input signal to the same system.
>
> **Transfer function** Mathematical representation of systems and sub-systems.
>
> **Summing point** Produces the algebraic sum of the reference signal and the feedback.

Transfer functions

Transfer functions represent system blocks mathematically (by using algebra). This helps with system modelling, analysis and fault finding. For example, see Figure 10.6.

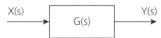

Figure 10.6 Transfer function example

$Y(s) = G(s)X(s)$, where $X(s)$ is the input signal and $Y(s)$ is the output signal.

Summing points

Summing points produce the algebraic sum of the reference signal and the feedback signal, resulting in an error signal, $E(s)$. For the example in Figure 10.7, where $E(s)$ is the error signal, $R(s)$ is the reference signal, $B(s)$ is the feedback signal and $C(s)$ is the output signal,

$E(s) = R(s) - B(s)$

The steady state error of a system is the difference between the desired output (the desired temperature in the heating systems example above) and the actual output (the actual temperature), measured when the control system has reached a steady state.

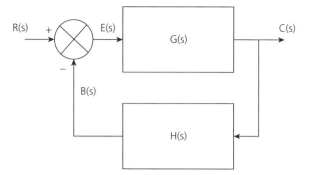

Figure 10.7 Summing point example

Pulse width and amplitude modulation

These are methods of converting signals into formats that are suitable for transmission. In pulse width modulation (PWM), the width of the pulsed carrier signal is varied according to the amplitude of the message signal.

In pulse amplitude modulation (PAM), the amplitude of the pulsed carrier signal is changed according to the amplitude of the message signal.

How control systems are represented in diagrams

Systems can be represented using different types of diagrams.
+ Block diagrams show a top-down overview of systems in terms of their input, process and output blocks.
+ Schematics show the individual components in a system as standard circuit symbols.
+ Wiring diagrams show the components as pictorial representations joined together by wires, as they will be arranged when placed *in situ*.

Applications of control systems

REVISED

Electrical control systems utilise electrical and electronic power supplies, components and signals. Through sensors they monitor parameters such as pressure level, flow rate, temperature, speed and position.

Pneumatic systems use compressed air as the transmission and power medium. These are used where accuracy and precision are required, for example, in braking and CNC machine control systems. Hydraulic systems use a liquid, such as oil or water. These are used where a large amount of power is required, for example in aircraft landing gears and heavy lifting equipment in the construction industry.

> **Revision activity**
>
> For a system you have studied (e.g. a timer or comparator system), produce a block diagram, schematic and wiring diagram. Explain the differences between the three diagrams and say why they are presented in the way that they are.

> **Typical mistake**
>
> System block diagrams are often drawn incorrectly. Make sure that you include input, process and output blocks, signal arrows and feedback as appropriate for the system.

> **Now test yourself**   TESTED
>
> 1 Give **two** examples of input devices.
> 2 Explain the function of a latching system.
> 3 Explain the purpose of transfer functions in control systems.
> 4 Define the term 'pulse width modulation' (PWM).
> 5 Outline the difference between pneumatic and hydraulic control systems.

> **Revision activity**
>
> Find and list examples of open- and closed-loop control systems. What are the differences between them and how do they work?

Check your understanding and progress at **www.hoddereducation.co.uk/myrevisionnotes**

10.2 How sensors and actuators are used in automation control systems

Sensors

Sensors detect changes in the environment around them.

Types of sensors include:
+ analogue sensors – these measure and/or produce analogue output signals
+ digital sensors – these measure and/or produce digital output signals
+ active sensors – these send a signal into the environment and measure the responses that they get back, for example infrared sensors send out infrared signals and wait for a response
+ passive sensors – these monitor changes in the environment without otherwise interfering with it, for example temperature sensors.

Applications of sensors include:
+ switching systems
+ measuring proximity to an object
+ using lasers to measure the dimensions of an object
+ vision systems.

> **Sensors** Devices that detect changes in the environment around them.

Actuators

Actuators are output devices. They produce physical movement in response to a received signal, e.g. a motor or solenoid. Active actuators require their own power supply, and/or are capable of introducing new energy into a system. Passive actuators do not need their own power supply and do not introduce any new energy into a system.

Both sensors and actuators can either be hard-wired into a system or operated wirelessly.

> **Actuators** Devices that produce physical movement in response to a received signal.

Uses in automation

Sensors and actuators are used in automated production and manufacturing systems, for example:
+ measuring the position and volume of objects being processed
+ measuring different parameters within a production environment, such as electrical, chemical, biological, optical, radiation and acoustic factors
+ lifting and moving objects from one workstation to another
+ robot arms and systems.

> **Exam tip**
>
> Make sure you know the differences between the types of sensors used in control systems.

Now test yourself

TESTED

6 Describe the function of a digital sensor.

7 Explain the difference between active and passive sensors.

8 Give **two** examples of actuators.

9 Describe **one** application of sensors in automated production systems.

10 Describe **one** application of actuators in automated production systems.

Summary

In this content area you learned about:

+ the input, process and output devices used in control systems
+ the differences between open- and closed-loop systems
+ the purpose of transfer functions and summing points
+ the purpose of pulse width and amplitude modulation
+ how control systems are represented
+ applications of control systems in engineering and manufacturing processes
+ the different types of sensors and actuators used in control systems, and their applications in automation.

Exam-style questions

1 Name **three** different types of logic gates. [3]

2 Describe the function of a timer in a control system. [2]

3 Describe the function of a comparator in a control system. [2]

4 Define the term 'analogue signal'. [1]

5 Explain how summing points are used in control systems. [4]

6 An engineer is designing a security lighting system to be installed on the outside of a building. Explain why they should produce both a wiring diagram and a schematic for this purpose. [6]

7 Define the term 'analogue actuator'. [1]

8 An engineer is designing an automated locking system for a materials store-room door. Identify an actuator that could move a lock into place when the door is closed and explain its function. [3]

9 Describe how an active sensor functions. [2]

10 A company is planning to build a new factory to mass produce electronic circuit boards for phones. Each of the assembly operations will be carried out by dedicated robotic arms. The factory will work seven days a week, 24 hours a day in order to meet demand. New phone designs will be manufactured each year. Explain why programmable logic controllers (PLCs) would be used to control the robotic arms, rather than dedicated integrated circuits. [6]

11 Quality management

11.1 Quality standards, assurance, control and improvement

The purpose of quality standards is to provide guidance on how organisations can comply with all applicable laws and regulations.

Quality standards:
+ are continuously updated to take advantage of the latest technological advances and ensure compliance with the latest legislation
+ provide recommendations for the design and manufacture of products, as well as setting minimum requirements
+ provide recommendations for design and manufacturing processes to ensure high levels of quality and safety
+ have been written and approved by engineering experts with specialised knowledge.

> **Compliance** Being in accordance with commands, rules or requests.
>
> **Legislation** A law or set of laws passed by Parliament.

Types of quality standards

REVISED

British standards

As the national standards body for the UK, the British Standards Institution (BSI) is responsible for developing standards. In addition to developing standards for the UK, it also collaborates with other international organisations.

Figure 11.1 BSI logo

European conformity (CE)

CE identifies products that meet the health, safety, and environmental protection standards for products sold within the European Economic Area (EEA). CE is the abbreviation for *conformité européenne* – European conformity.

International Organization for Standardization (ISO)

This is a global organisation dedicated to the development of standards to ensure the quality, safety and efficiency of products and services that are available internationally. The ISO covers a large number of areas, from product manufacture and technology to healthcare, agriculture and food safety standards.

Roles and responsibilities of engineering bodies

REVISED

To ensure the safety of the public, professional engineering institutions are licensed by the Engineering Council to assess and register graduate and professional engineers and technicians, and govern their conduct and continuing development. There are a number of professional engineering institutions in the UK (Table 11.1).

Table 11.1 Roles and responsibilities of engineering bodies

Engineering body	What they do
Institution of Engineering and Technology (IET)	This body promotes the exchange of information and ideas for the advancement of science, engineering and technology worldwide. It shares expertise with the UK government; provides a range of professional services and products to support engineers throughout their careers; and champions engineering to inspire the next generation of engineers and technologists.
Institution of Mechanical Engineers (IMechE)	This body provides mechanical engineers with knowledge and skills in mechanical engineering across the globe. Strategic partnerships with leading multinational organisations enable it to train technical workforces to the highest standards.
Society of Operations Engineers (SOE)	This is a professional body for people who inspect, maintain, and manage equipment and machinery at work.
Chartered Institution of Building Services Engineers (CIBSE)	This body offers a wide range of courses to assist building services engineers to attain professional registration and membership. Building accounts for almost 50% of all harmful carbon emissions, so CIBSE works with engineers to make buildings more energy efficient.
Institution of Agricultural Engineers (IAgrE)	This body is a professional membership association with interests in agriculture, forestry, the environment, horticulture, amenities and forestry. Academics, engineers and industry bodies come together to improve technology in this field.
The Welding Institute (TWI)	This body aims to ensure that engineering companies value welding and joining professionals. There is a strong commitment to the professional development of welders and joiners, and to their safety.

The Institute of the Motor Industry (IMI) is not an Engineering Council licensed institution but does develop skills benchmarks for engineers and technicians in the automotive industry. The IMI training programme includes training on new technologies, such as electric vehicles (EVs) and hydrogen fuel cell electric vehicles (FCEVs).

Figure 11.2 Institute of the Motor Industry logo

Now test yourself   TESTED

1. What does the acronym ISO stand for?
2. Which engineering body is responsible for agricultural engineers in the UK?
3. What does the acronym BSI stand for?
4. Who issues the CE mark?

Exam tip

For each engineering body, ensure that you can state at least one main responsibility.

Typical mistake

Do not confuse legislation with compliance. Legislation is a set of laws and compliance is following the law.

Revision activity

Create a mind map of all the different engineering bodies within the United Kingdom Add one key point to each body to state what their main purposes are.

Quality assurance (QA) and quality control (QC)   REVISED

Culture of quality

Culture of quality refers to an environment in which all employees are responsible for and actively contributes to quality. Quality guidelines should not be followed blindly by organisations, but discussed constantly at all levels. One test, one tool or one person is not enough to guarantee quality. Everyone needs to commit to making it happen.

Figure 11.3 Quality assurance and quality control

Check your understanding and progress at **www.hoddereducation.co.uk/myrevisionnotes**

The difference between QA and QC

Defects and mistakes in manufactured products are prevented through quality assurance. It is a management approach that ensures quality standards and customer requirements are met.

Quality control is about making sure that the product meets the accepted standard by detection.

> **Detection** The action of identifying something which may be hidden.

Table 11.2 Quality assurance and quality control comparison

Quality assurance (QA)	Quality control (QC)
A proactive approach to management	A reactive corrective measure
Process-centred	Product-centred
Ensures defects are prevented	Defects are detected
All employees in an organisation are responsible	The testing department has the responsibility
Processed during manufacturing	Once the product has been manufactured, it is tested

Quality assurance approaches

Quality assurance follows guidelines from standards and uses various systems and approaches to achieve it:

+ Total quality management (TQM)
+ Right first time
+ Quality standards (ISO 90001 – Quality management systems)
+ Traceability
+ Inspection and testing
+ Document management and version control.

Table 11.3 Quality assurance approaches

QA approach	Purpose and outcome of testing
Total quality management (TQM)	TQM is a continual process that aims to: + detect and reduce manufacturing errors + enhance supply-chain management + increase customer satisfaction + train employees as needed.
Right first time	Producing products efficiently and reducing waste requires that any procedure is done the right way the first time.
Quality standards (ISO 9001 – Quality management systems)	ISO 9001 is an international standard that defines the requirements for quality management systems. Business organisations can benefit from it by becoming more efficient and improving customer satisfaction. Implementing ISO 9001 reduces costs by improving productivity and efficiency, contributes to increased sales, repeat business and additional income, increases the reputation of a company and attracts new customers.
Traceability	The goal of traceability is to identify and track all processes within an organisation, including the purchase of raw materials, manufacturing and disposal. An easily identifiable source (and other information about a component, e.g. the batch number) is essential. As each component or material is used, a record of that transaction should be attached, including the batch number, date and time.
Inspection and testing	Inspection is conducted to ensure raw materials and components purchased by an organisation meet a standard, such as quality, before use in production. Testing is conducted during quality control checks to ensure that manufactured products meet the tolerances. If a product fails to meet this standard, it will be rejected. Corrective measures will be implemented to ensure that future products all meet this standard.

5 Which international standard sets out the requirements for a quality management system?

6 What does the acronym TQM stand for?

7 Describe the term 'quality assurance'.

8 Why is document and version control important?

9 Why is right first time (RFT) used in quality management?

DMAIC A data-driven problem-solving method to help identify and fix problems within a process and improve future output.

Exam tip

Make sure you can remember the six main quality assurance approaches and can describe each one.

Typical mistake

Do not confuse quality assurance and quality control. Quality assurance is a management system to prevent error and mistakes in products while quality control is the physical checking of products to make sure they are up to standard.

Specification limits The values that define whether a product works or not. They assess how capable a process is of meeting the customer requirements.

Purpose of inspection

The purpose of inspection is to:

+ identify acceptable lots (batches) from unacceptable ones
+ determine whether the process is changing
+ determine whether the product or process is approaching the specification limits
+ determine the quality of a product
+ assess inspectors' accuracy
+ determine the accuracy of the measuring instrument (see Figure 11.4).
+ measure process efficiency.

Revision activity

Research and draw a diagram to show the four basic categories of total quality management (TQM).

Figure 11.4 Inspection is important for verifying the precision of measuring instruments

Stages of inspection

1 Before raw materials and components are placed in stock or used in production, they are tested to ensure their suitability.

2 At critical points in the production process, sampling and inspection are necessary. When errors occur, the production stage can be identified and appropriate action taken.

3 Final products are inspected before they are released. When a product does not meet standards, it may be rejected or sold for a lower price.

Sampling The process of selecting batches of products to test.

Types of inspection

An inspection can be carried out in two ways:
+ 100% sampling inspection
+ statistical process control (SPC) – sampling inspection.

100% sampling inspection

Using a 100% sampling technique, every part of a product or component is examined separately.

Process capability

Figure 11.6 shows a customer's manufacturing limits for a product. There is a nominal height measurement of 5 mm, a lower specification limit (LSL) measurement of 4.98 mm and an upper specification limit (USL) measurement of 5.02 mm. A histogram was generated based on the results of testing 100 products. The process was deemed capable after 96% of the products passed the specification limits.

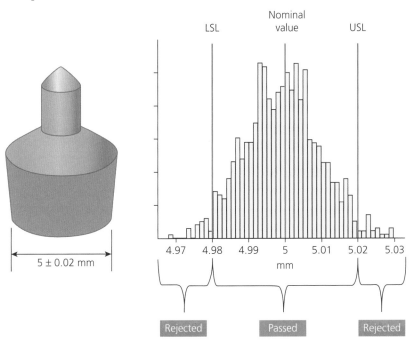

Figure 11.6 Process capability diagram

Statistical process control

A statistical process control (SPC) method measures, monitors and controls a process using statistical methods. The system ensures that manufacturing processes are efficient, resulting in less waste, and detects problems early, allowing changes to be made before products have been manufactured.

Control charts are often used in SPC. Figure 11.7 shows how the dimensions of a product sample can change over time. Average output is represented by the centre line. The lower control limit (LCL) shows the lower tolerance limit and the upper control limit (UCL) shows the upper tolerance limit.

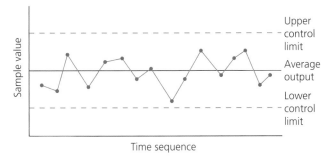

Figure 11.7 SPC control chart

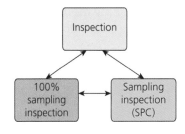

Figure 11.5 Types of inspection

> **Histogram** A graphical chart that displays data using bars of different heights. It groups the data into ranges and the height of each bar shows how many are in each range.
>
> **Testing** Sample batches are checked to ensure they are within the customer's specifications for the final product. This determines whether any corrective actions are needed in the manufacturing process.

My Revision Notes: Engineering and Manufacturing T Level

The sampling method used for high-value and safety-critical products is 100% sampling inspection. In high-speed manufacturing, SPC is typically used.

Figure 11.8 shows the comparison of 100% sampling versus statistical process control (SPC).

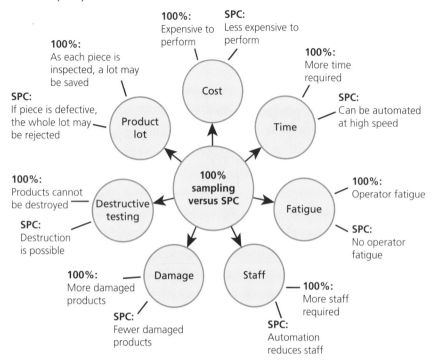

Figure 11.8 Comparison of 100% sampling versus statistical process control

Six Sigma

Six Sigma refers to an approach used in high volume manufacturing, where the tolerance limits for any features take into account the process capabilities and are designed to be within three standard deviations each way of the nominal value. Therefore almost all parts are made correctly, reducing costs of scrap and inspection requirements. Six Sigma implementation may involve design work to determine the tolerances within which a product will function as intended and improvements in process capability.

> **Six Sigma** A set of quality management techniques that aim to improve the processes within an organisation to greatly reduce the amount of manufacturing errors and product defects.

Quality improvement

Quality improvement is the systematic process of improving quality using specific methods and tools. Improvements in quality can be modelled by the PDSA (plan, do, study, act cycle shown in Figure 11.9).

Failure mode effect analysis (FMEA)

Failure mode effect analysis (FMEA) is a structured method for identifying and dealing with potential problems, or systemic failures and their consequences. When it comes to a process, consider what could possibly go wrong.

Figure 11.9 PDSA cycle

Table 11.4 The advantages and disadvantages of FMEA

Advantages	Disadvantages
Allows prioritisation of actions	The evaluation process can vary from team to team
An effective communication tool	A time-consuming process
Can be applied to both existing and new products	Evaluations are often subjective
Determines how much risk and action are involved	Can be impossible to manage solutions that are so large and complex

Check your understanding and progress at **www.hoddereducation.co.uk/myrevisionnotes**

Quality circles

In quality circles, employees from different levels within the organisation come together to discuss and solve production-related problems. Figure 11.10 shows the advantages and disadvantages of quality circles.

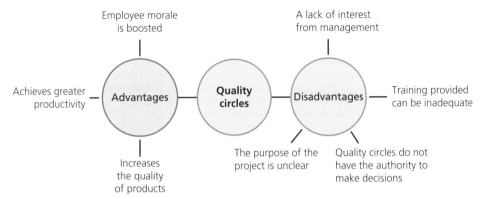

Figure 11.10 The advantages and disadvantages of quality circles

Pareto analysis

The Pareto analysis helps a manufacturer to identify different solutions to a problem before selecting the most suitable one. The Pareto principle states that for many incidents, roughly 80% of consequences can be traced back to 20% of causes.

For example, 80% of decisions in a meeting are made in 20% of the time; 80% of pollution originates from 20% of all factories. Figure 11.11 shows the advantages and disadvantages of quality circles.

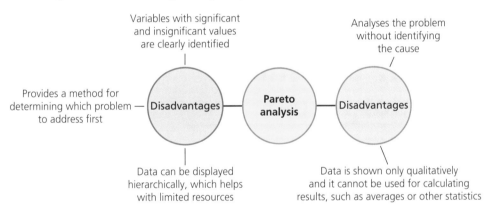

Figure 11.11 The advantages and disadvantages of Pareto analysis

Cause and effect diagrams

Cause and effect diagrams, also known as Ishikawa diagrams or fishbone diagrams, are used to explore the possible causes of a certain event (see Figure 11.12).

Diagrams help identify the root causes of a problem statement by categorising the causes into discrete branches.

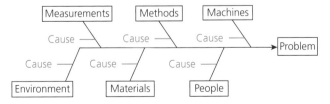

Figure 11.12 Cause and effect diagram

> **Exam tip**
>
> Remember that there are two main types of inspection: 100% sampling inspection and statistical process control (SPC) sampling inspection.

> **Typical mistake**
>
> For each type of inspection try to remember two advantages and two disadvantages.

Revision activity

You been asked, by your supervisor, to create a SPC control chart for a sample of eight pieces from the manufacturing line.

a   Add the following measurements to a copy of the chart in Figure 11.13.

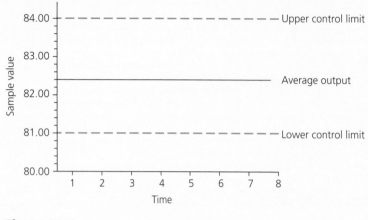

Figure 11.13

Time 1 = 81.40	Time 5 = 83.00
Time 2 = 81.80	Time 6 = 80.80
Time 3 = 81.80	Time 7 = 83.80
Time 4 = 82.60	Time 8 = 82.20

b   State which measurement does not meet the control limits.

c   Which measurements are nearest to the average output?

11.2 Types and applications of standard operating procedures (SOPs) and their purposes

A standard operating procedure (SOP) describes the steps employees need to follow to ensure that all processes are completed to the standard expected by the organisation. The purpose of an SOP is to standardise activities, assure customer satisfaction, specify safe working practices or as a training tool.

SOPs consist of clear, step-by-step procedures and checklists. The goal is to reduce the possibility of making mistakes. They are commonly used for:
+ manufacturing
+ quality assurance and control
+ maintenance.

Typical formats and content

REVISED ⬤

Typically, SOPs come in three formats:
+ step-by-step   + hierarchical   + flowchart.

> **Hierarchical** Ranked in order of importance.

Step-by-step SOPs

A step-by-step SOP identifies each step in the process and breaks it down into a numbered list. All steps should be clear enough that they can be followed without supervision.

For example, a step-by-step SOP for the pre-operational safety checks for an angle grinder might include:

Check your understanding and progress at **www.hoddereducation.co.uk/myrevisionnotes**

1 Ensure training is up to date.
2 Keep work area clean and tidy.
3 Use only in a designated grinding area – erect screens if necessary.
4 Examine the power cord, extension lead, sockets and power outage for damage.
5 Ensure that the grinding disc, guard and attachments are secure and correctly fitted.

Hierarchical SOPs

Hierarchical SOPs are used for more complex procedures with many steps (see Figure 11.14).

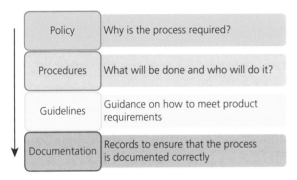

Figure 11.14 Hierarchical SOP diagram

Flowchart SOPs

Flowchart SOPs represent processes or workflows in diagrammatic form.
They guide you from start to finish by providing a visual method for completing a process (see Figure 11.15).

Production of SOPs

Figure 11.16 outlines how SOPs are produced.

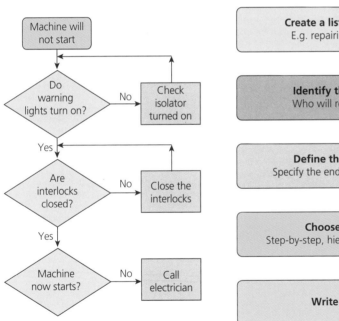

Figure 11.15 Flowchart SOP diagram   **Figure 11.16** Production of SOPs

> **Revision activity**
>
> Write a step-by-step SOP for the operation of a machine of your choice. Include the following:
> + title
> + list of equipment and materials needed
> + potential hazards
> + skills required
> + number of personnel needed
> + time needed to complete
> + recommended frequency for completing the task
> + steps to follow.

> **Now test yourself**   TESTED ⬤
>
> 10 What is the Pareto principle?
> 11 What is a cause and effect diagram used for?
> 12 What does UCL mean on a quality control chart?
> 13 Name one format of standard operating procedures (SOPs).
> 14 What does the acronym SPC stand for?

Summary

In this content area you learned about:

+ quality standards, assurance, control and improvement
+ types and applications of standard operating procedures (SOPs) and their purposes.

Exam-style questions

1 Name **one** inspection technique. [1]

2 Define the acronym BSI. [1]

3 Describe the term 'standards'. [1]

4 Define the term 'quality assurance'. [1]

5 Name the engineering body that represents vehicle manufacturers in the UK. [1]

6 State the rule that is also known as the Pareto principle. [1]

7 Describe what a cause and effect diagram is used for. [1]

8 Explain the purpose of the International Organization for Standardization (ISO). [2]

9 Describe the main purpose of the engineering body CIBSE. [2]

10 Define the term 'traceability'. [3]

11 Name **two** purposes of inspection. [2]

12 Identify **two** purposes of document version control. [2]

13 Name **two** stages in the production of a standard operating procedure (SOP). [2]

14 Explain, with **one** example, the benefit of using Six Sigma in manufacturing. [2]

15 Give **one** advantage and **two** disadvantages of quality circles. [3]

16 Discuss the advantages and disadvantages of 100% sampling compared to statistical process control (SPC). [6]

17 Explain why companies use SOPs. [4]

12 Health and safety principles and coverage

12.1 The main requirements of key health and safety legislation applicable to engineering activities

Health and safety legislation protects employers, employees and anyone else who may be exposed to hazards at work. The law places obligations on various duty holders to reduce or eliminate the risk of harm.

Engineering in the UK is governed by many different laws, including health, safety and welfare laws. Legislation is made up of Acts of Parliament and regulations (statutory legislation), which must be followed to avoid prosecution.

> **Hazard** Anything that has the potential to cause harm.
>
> **Duty holder** A person who is legally responsible.

Legislation

 REVISED

All companies must follow health and safety legislation to protect their employees. The main requirements of the current key legislation are listed in Table 12.1. Government agencies publish legislation changes and these can be accessed through regulatory bodies, such as the Health and Safety Executive (HSE) at www.hse.gov.uk and also www.legislation.gov.uk.

Table 12.1 Key health and safety legislation

Legislation	Main requirements
The Health and Safety at Work Act (HASAWA)	Employers must: + protect people's health, safety and welfare at work + ensure the safety and health of people outside the workplace (for example, visitors or the general public) + be in control of explosives, highly flammable substances or other potentially hazardous materials.
Management of Health and Safety at Work Regulations (MHSWR)	Employers must: + undertake a **risk assessment** and record significant findings if there are five or more employees + appoint competent people to support health and safety measures + establish emergency procedures.
Provision and Use of Work Equipment Regulations (PUWER)	Employers must ensure: + work equipment is safe for use + equipment operators are trained + work equipment is correctly maintained.
Personal Protective Equipment (PPE) Regulations	Employers should ensure PPE is: + fit for purpose + correctly stored + maintained + used properly by operators.
The Control of Noise at Work Regulations	Employers must: + carry out a risk assessment if noise levels reach 80 decibels, in order to control exposure + provide PPE and noise-control equipment.
Manual Handling Operations Regulations	Employers should: + avoid requiring employees to perform hazardous manual-handling tasks. + conduct a risk assessment if they cannot be avoided.

111

Legislation	Main requirements
Lifting Operations and Lifting Equipment Regulations (LOLER)	Employers must ensure **lifting operations** are: + planned by a competent person + supervised appropriately + safely carried out.
Work at Height Regulations	Employers must ensure: + work at height is organised and properly planned. + those working at height are competent + a risk assessment is conducted and appropriate work equipment is selected + risks of working near or on fragile surfaces are managed.
Electricity at Work Regulations	Employers must ensure: + electrical systems are designed to prevent danger + a five-year inspection is performed on electrical systems + electrical work is performed safely + only trained and competent employees work with electrical equipment.
The Control of Electromagnetic Fields at Work Regulations (CEMFAW)	Employers must risk assess the levels of electromagnetic fields (EMFs) to which their employees may be exposed. EMFs include X-rays, gamma rays and high-energy ultraviolet (UV) rays.
Reporting of Injuries, Diseases and Dangerous Occurrences Regulations (RIDDOR)	Employers must report and keep records under RIDDOR for: + work-related fatalities and serious injuries (reportable injuries) + 'dangerous occurrences' (incidents that can cause harm) + diagnosed cases of industrial diseases.
Control of Substances Hazardous to Health Regulations (COSHH)	Employers must: + assess risks of hazardous substances at work + monitor the exposure of employees to hazardous substances + provide training to employees who may be exposed to hazardous substances + make plans for emergencies involving hazardous substances.

Risk assessment Method of identifying and evaluating hazards to determine whether control measures are sufficient to prevent harm.

Personal protective equipment (PPE) Clothing or equipment designed to protect a user from workplace hazards.

Lifting operation An operation concerned with the lifting or lowering of a load.

Health and safety culture

Workplace health and safety is defined by both the safety management system, and the health and safety culture. In other words, the shared values, beliefs, expectations and attitudes about safe behaviour.

Exam tip

Examiners may ask you for the main requirements of statutory legislation. Make sure you can remember at least two main requirements of each Act and regulation.

Typical mistake

Do not confuse manual handling operations and lifting operations. Manual handling involves people handling loads while lifting operations use lifting equipment for heavy loads.

Revision activity

Research the Health and Safety at Work Act (HASAWA) and make a list of which people the Act relates to at work. What are the duties of the employer under the Act?

Check your understanding and progress at **www.hoddereducation.co.uk/myrevisionnotes**

12.2 The importance of health and safety practices within the workplace

The impact of legislation on accidents and related incidents

If health and safety legislation is followed by a company, there is likely to be:
+ improvement in the company's reputation
+ increased productivity
+ lower insurance premiums
+ reduced staff turnover
+ reduced employee absenteeism
+ fewer accidents and therefore a reduction in legal claims.

In 2018, the UK had the lowest standardised incidence ratio (SIR) of fatal workplace injuries among large EU economies (prior to the UK leaving the EU). This illustrates the effectiveness of the UK's health and safety legislation.

RIDDOR reports assist the Health and Safety Executive in keeping track of common workplace injuries and safety regulations.

The most frequent non-fatal injuries to employees are shown in the chart below.

> **Standardised incidence ratio (SIR)** An estimate of the number of cases in a given population compared to what might be predicted based on a comparison with the experience in a larger population.

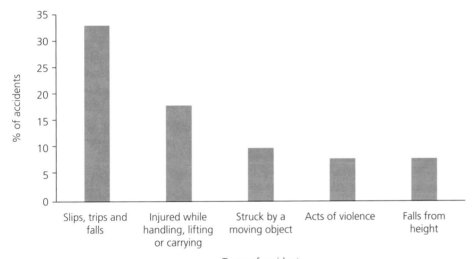

Figure 12.1 Type of workplace accident occurring in Great Britain in 2021 (Contains public sector information published by the Health and Safety Executive and licensed under the Open Government Licence)

Using this legislation, the Health and Safety Executive can assess the effectiveness of the legislation on the frequency and severity of accidents and injuries in organisations.

Mental health and wellbeing in the workplace

Emotional, psychological and social wellbeing are all part of mental health. A person's thinking, feeling and acting are affected by it. Anxiety and depression are the most common mental health issues.

In some cases, they are caused by:
+ incidents resulting in severe injuries, death or threats of death
+ bereavement or divorce, and other life challenges
+ workplace stress.

113

Compliance with health and safety legislation

REVISED

The Health and Safety at Work Act (HASAWA) applies to everyone at work. Employers, employees, self-employed individuals, suppliers of workplace materials and others are all duty holders.

Legislation specifically targets people in the workplace, rather than premises or processes.

Provisions in the Act protect employees and other members of the public who may be at risk due to workplace activities.

In the UK, there are two main branches of law, criminal law and civil law:
+ Criminal law maintains law and order and protects society. Employers who breach health and safety regulations may be prosecuted by the Health and Safety Executive or a local authority.
+ Civil law protects the rights of individual victims. Workers who are injured at work may sue their employer for compensation.

Enforcing authorities

Health and Safety Executive (HSE)

Health and safety legislation in Great Britain is enforced either by the Health and Safety Executive (HSE) or a local authority (LA) depending on the main activity at the location.

In general, LAs enforce retail, wholesale distribution, warehousing, offices, and consumer or leisure properties.

Health and safety inspectors can carry out a variety of health and safety actions, such as:
+ performing workplace inspections
+ issuing formal and informal legal notices to duty holders
+ taking action to prosecute.

Implications of non-compliance

REVISED

Health and safety risks need to be managed and legislation must be followed. If not, HSE can take enforcement action against individuals and businesses.

While inspecting, inspectors may give informal verbal or written advice about minor issues, allowing duty holders to resolve issues before formal action is taken. If a serious breach of HASAWA is discovered, an inspector may:
+ issue an improvement notice specifying what to do in order to comply with the law, why, and within what timeframe (usually 21 days to allow the duty holder time to appeal)
+ prohibit activities that pose a serious risk of personal injury (either immediately or after a specified period of time); this prohibition will not be lifted until the cause has been corrected
+ file criminal charges in court.

> **Typical mistake**
>
> Make sure you know the difference between criminal and civil law. Criminal law protects society and civil law protects the individual.

> **Revision activity**
>
> Consider this scenario and decide what actions may be taken.
>
> During the descent of two steps on the side of a water tank, an employee slipped and fell. Although known to get wet, the steps were made from standard floor plate. The employee dislocated their shoulder and was away from work for several weeks.

> **Exam tip**
>
> Examiners may ask you what powers enforcing authorities have. Make sure you know how health and safety inspectors can enforce the law.

> **Now test yourself**
>
> TESTED
>
> 1 What piece of legislation ensures the safety of machinery and tools?
> 2 What types of notices can an HSE inspector issue?
> 3 What piece of legislation covers moving or carrying a load?
> 4 What does the abbreviation COSHH mean?
> 5 What does the acronym HSE stand for?

Check your understanding and progress at **www.hoddereducation.co.uk/myrevisionnotes**

12.3 Responsibilities for health and safety

Under the HASAWA, employers and employees have key responsibilities while at work. These are detailed in Table 12.2.

Table 12.2 Employer and employee responsibilities

Health and safety responsibilities of employees	Health and safety responsibilities of employers
+ work safely so as not to cause injury to self and others in the vicinity + not to attempt any work task unless trained and authorised to do so + co-operate with the employer to enable the duties placed on the employer to be performed + have regard of any duty or requirement imposed upon the employer or any other person under any of the statutory provisions + not interfere with or misuse anything provided in the interests of health, safety or welfare	+ minimising risks in the handling, storage and transport of articles and substances + instruction, training and supervision to maintain high standards of health and safety at work + maintaining the workplace and its environment to be safe and minimising risk to health + to provide a statement of general health and safety policy + provide arrangements for safety representatives and safety committees + ensure the safety of visitors, contractors and members of the public

Local, national and global requirements

 REVISED

Local

The HSE enforces safety legislation in the UK, along with local authorities.

Table 12.3 Local health and safety in the UK

HSE	Responsible for agricultural, construction, medical, education and manufacturing.
	Among these are factories, farms, construction sites, hospitals, nursing homes and schools.
Local authorities	Sectors include retail, wholesale distribution, hospitality, catering, beauty and leisure.
	These include stores, offices, warehouses, hotels, pubs, restaurants, hotels, hairdressers, nail salons, health clubs, theatres and cinemas.

National

The Health and Safety Executive provides advice, information and guidance on health and safety at work in the UK.

Global

Around the world, different approaches are taken to health and safety.

In developing countries, health and safety at work is often not prioritised, and legislation can be lacking. Without legal protection, occupational injuries and diseases are common. The conditions of work are unsafe for those living in poverty. In contrast, countries in Europe, the US and Canada tend to strictly enforce their health and safety regulations.

> **Exam tip**
>
> Make sure you understand the difference between local, national and global health and safety requirements.

12.4 Risk assessment

Hazards in engineering and manufacturing

Among the main hazards associated with engineering and manufacturing are:
+ equipment and tools – noise, vibration, manual handling, machinery safeguarding
+ stored energy – electrical shock risk from non-isolated equipment
+ electricity – risk of electrocution
+ harmful substances, including gases – fluids and solvents used in metalworking, dust and fumes from welding, brazing, soldering, and coating and painting
+ environments – order and cleanliness are important in the workplace, including areas for work and storage.

Risk assessment

The purpose of a risk assessment is to identify work-related hazards and to implement control measures to eliminate or reduce the risk of harm.

Stages of risk assessment

HSE recommend a three-step assessment process:
1 Identify potential hazards (see 'Hazard identification (HAZID)' below).
2 Assess who may be harmed and how. How will the workplace, equipment, and processes be accessed, and what hazards will be encountered?
3 Identify the risks and implement control measures.

Hazard identification (HAZID)

The first stage in assessing risks is HAZID. It identifies activities that have the potential to cause harm. Engineering and manufacturing activities may give rise to the following hazards:
+ machines that are not guarded
+ tool and equipment noise and vibration
+ non-isolated equipment that stores energy
+ electrical equipment that is not maintained or is defective
+ the misuse of electrical equipment
+ inhalation of harmful substances and gases
+ poor housekeeping resulting in slips, trips and falls
+ dangerous working conditions (e.g. working in confined spaces).

Common industrial injuries that can occur without appropriate precautions include:
+ the flow of people, goods, and vehicles through the workshop causing slips, trips and collisions
+ manual handling of heavy loads causing cuts, sprains and bruises and musculoskeletal injuries
+ machinery safeguarding causing entanglement, cuts and burns.
+ metalworking fluids, degreasing solvents, dust and fumes produced when welding, brazing, soldering, coatings, and painting are hazardous substances. These can cause skin and lung damage.
+ excessive noise can cause hearing problems and deafness
+ excessive vibration can cause hand arm vibration syndrome (HAVS)

Hazard and operability study (HAZOP)

HAZOP identifies and evaluates hazards for a specific operation, such as the operation of a machine or automated process. It allows for the detection of practical maintenance issues as well as significant problems with operation and quality. Figure 12.2 shows the HAZOP process.

> **Material Safety Data Sheet (MSDS)** An important information source to help eliminate or reduce the risks associated with hazardous chemicals and substances.

Figure 12.2 HAZOP process

Evaluation of risks

After hazards have been identified, each should be assessed for its level of risk. Risk levels are commonly assessed by assigning scores based on how likely it is that harm will occur and how severe it may be. The scores are multiplied together to produce a risk rating, which can be read on a risk matrix.

For example, the likelihood of a hazard may be scored 1–5, where:
1 Rarely occurs
2 Unlikely to occur
3 May possibly occur
4 Likely to occur
5 Certain to occur

Severity of injury may also be scored 1–5, where:
1 represents negligible (for example, an injury where no first aid is required)
2 represents minor (for example, an injury where minor first aid is required)
3 represents moderate (for example, a serious injury that requires medical assistance and must be reported)
4 represents significant (for example, a serious injury requiring urgent medical assistance or hospitalisation)
5 represents severe (usually a fatality).

Figure 12.3 uses these figures to determine risk levels as low (green), medium-low (yellow), medium-high (orange) or high (red).

Consequences/impact	Catastrophic	5	5	10	15	20	25
	Major	4	4	8	12	16	20
	Moderate	3	3	6	9	12	15
	Minor	2	2	4	6	8	10
	Insignificant	1	1	2	3	4	5
			1	2	3	4	5
			Rare	Unlikely	Possible	Likely	Almost certain
			Likelihood/probability				

Figure 12.3 Risk matrix table

Hierarchy of control

Control measures should be identified during a risk assessment that either eliminate or reduce the likelihood of a hazard causing harm. As a result of the hierarchy of control, control measures are categorised according to how effective they are at reducing risk. Figure 12.4 describes the hierarchy of control.

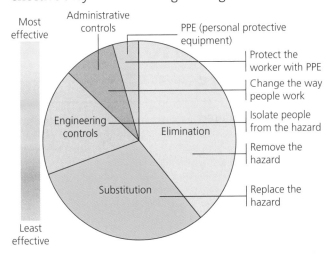

Figure 12.4 Hierarchy of control diagram

Typical control measures in engineering

The following control measures are typically used in engineering:

+ isolation of machinery
+ use of guards on machines
+ personal protective equipment (PPE) that includes:
    + respiratory protection, i.e. face masks and respirators
    + eye protection
    + safety shoes for foot protection
    + ear protection using ear muffs
    + gauntlets and gloves
    + hard helmets.

Now test yourself

TESTED ○

6 What is the correct sequence for risk assessment?
7 What item of PPE protects the lungs?
8 Who should provide an employee with PPE?
9 What does the acronym HAZID mean?

Revision activity

Copy and complete the mind map in Figure 12.5 to identify hazards associated with activities that have the potential to cause harm within engineering and manufacturing.

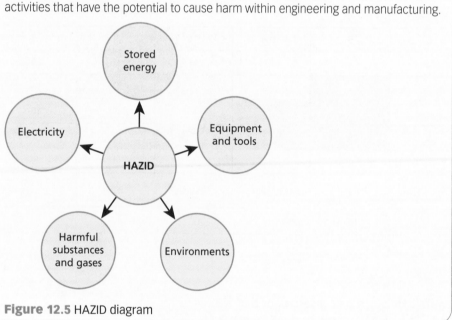

Figure 12.5 HAZID diagram

12.5 Health and safety considerations in specific engineering contexts

In engineering, a number of processes and operations need to be considered to ensure health and safety.

Spontaneous combustion A substance unexpectedly bursts into flame without apparent cause.

Asphyxiation Process of being deprived of oxygen, which can result in unconsciousness or death; suffocation.

Table 12.4 Health and safety operations and processes

Operations and processes	
Safe systems of work (SSoW)	An operation's set of procedures that eliminates or minimises its risks. These systems must be adhered to by everyone.
Permit to work (PTW)	When work is considered to be high risk, PTW authorises certain people to perform certain tasks within a certain time limit. PTWs are required for the following types of work: + performing 'hot works', such as welding and plasma cutting + working in confined spaces, such as in a tank + working alone, for example in sewers or tanks + machinery and equipment maintenance, for example maintenance of a welder.
Oxygen use in the workplace	Be aware of the dangers of oxygen as it is a highly reactive gas that can cause fires and explosions. Do no smoke where oxygen is being used. Do not use oil and grease to lubricate cylinders and equipment as it can react destructively with pure oxygen at high pressures. Prevent oxygen enrichment by ensuring equipment is leak-tight as enrichment may cause some materials to catch fire spontaneously, for example **spontaneous combustion** of oily rags.
Fires and explosion hazards	Consider potential causes of fire and explosion: + electrical faults + overheating machinery and equipment + sparks from equipment + smoking materials + electrically overloaded circuits + static electricity + heaters and radiated heat. Consider storage of flammable and explosive substances: + grease, oil, fuels and other combustible materials + pressurised bottled gas.
Asphyxiation hazards	Asphyxiation can occur from some gases used in engineering therefore good ventilation is required. Hydrogen, methane and nitrogen are odourless asphyxiants that are not poisonous, but pose health risks. A common chemical asphyxiant is carbon monoxide, which is fatal when inhaled. Hydrogen sulfide is also a deadly gas if inhaled. Both are typically colourless and odourless.
Heat	A hot working environment can cause heat stress at the following workplaces: + manufacturing facilities for glass and rubber + mines and tunnels with compressed air + all types of power stations, including nuclear and conventional + foundry and smelting industries + plants that fire bricks and produce ceramics. To prevent heat stress considerations should be given to: + Controlling the temperature by using fans or air conditioning + Preventing dehydration by providing workers cool water + Using appropriate personal protective equipment such as clothing and respiratory protective equipment. + Allowing workers to acclimatise to their hot environments
Moving parts	Moving machine parts can cause injuries in the following ways: + moving parts of machinery or ejected materials can strike and injure people + body parts or clothing can get caught between rollers, belts or pulleys + severe injuries can result from sharp edges + sharp or pointed parts can stab or puncture the skin + abrasion or friction injuries can occur as a result of rough surfaces + a machine, wall or other object can crush a person, either between moving parts or against a fixed part. Therefore, consider preventing access to dangerous parts by using fixed guards.

Operations and processes	
Fire safety	Engineering workplace fires may be caused by: + overloaded plugs, loose wires and faulty connections (electrical fires), this is preventable by regular inspections of electrical equipment + accumulation of dust and grease can create a fire hazard therefore ensure good housekeeping and keep work areas clean + dirt and dust on machinery can also cause it to overheat, this is preventable by regular cleaning and maintenance + incorrect storage of combustible materials such as paper, cardboard and wood. It is recommended to store these in locked containers or to dispose of them regularly off-site.
Guarding	The main types of machine guarding are: + fixed; i.e. a barrier permanently attached to the machine + interlock; in this type of guard, the tripping mechanism and power are shut off if the guard is opened or removed + adjustable; a guard can adjust to fit a variety of products and be used with stock of various sizes + self-adjustable; a guard protects the operator by placing a barrier between them and the danger area. Consider the most appropriate guarding system to protect workers from accidental access to machinery.
Manual handling	The best way to reduce the risk of injury is to receive training that ensures correct posture and handling techniques.
Lock out tag out (LOTO) **Figure 12.6** Lock out tag out	In order to ensure the safety of maintenance work, hazardous energy sources must be isolated before maintenance can be performed. This ensures that workers are protected from injury or death caused by the unintentional release of stored energy during maintenance and repairs. The energy source is 'locked out' once it is turned off by a safety lock to prevent it from being powered back on. This device is then 'tagged out' so others cannot turn it on. Among these energy sources are: + electrical and mechanical + hydraulic and pneumatic + chemical + thermal energy and radiation.
High-voltage electrical	Always work safely by establishing safe procedures and considering the following: Earthing devices should only be used when there is no danger of electrocution + Always be cautious when working near high-voltage power lines + Ensure that exposed high-voltage equipment is kept at the recommended safety distance + Training and supervision should be provided as necessary.
Maintenance	The Provision and Use of Work Equipment 1998 Regulations (PUWER) requires employers to ensure that their work equipment is maintained in a safe and efficient manner to ensure that it does not deteriorate and place people at risk. Inspecting, cleaning, lubricating and making minor adjustments can prevent machinery shutdowns and ensure machinery safety. Considerations should be given to the following: Ensure the maintenance is covered by a SSoW + Is a PTW required to assess the risks on the maintenance activity to be used? + What are the safe means of access and egress from the areas where the maintenance is being carried out + Does the machine need isolating? This is to prevent injury from electrical, hydraulic or mechanical systems. + What other hazards are there to consider e.g. noise, heat, fumes or sharp edges? Ensure correct personal protective equipment is used. + Will the removal of parts expose live electrical wiring and parts? Ensure temporary cover are fitted to guard the exposed areas.

Check your understanding and progress at **www.hoddereducation.co.uk/myrevisionnotes**

12.6 Principles and practices relating to environmental legislation and considerations

Environmental legislation

REVISED

Environmental legislation protects the air, water and soil from pollution. Complying with the law is the employer's responsibility. Environmental policy and legislation in England are developed by the Department for Environment, Food and Rural Affairs (DEFRA). Table 12.5 shows the key environmental legislation.

Table 12.5 Environmental legislation

Environmental legislation	Key requirements
Environmental Protection Act 1990	Recycling and non-recycling waste should be separated on site or in a sorting plant. Registered waste carriers must collect waste or dispose of it directly. Records of waste transfer must be maintained for a minimum of two years.
Pollution Prevention and Control Act 1999	High pollution activities need an environmental permit, covering such areas as: + waste + air and water quality + sound pollution from the environment.
Clean Air Act (CAA) 2022	Regulates emissions, chimney height, and fuel content and composition. There is a prohibition on **dark smoke** coming from chimneys or flues in industrial premises. Burning materials on site also falls under this category
Radioactive Substances Act 1993	The control and disposal of radioactive material. Radioactive materials must: + be tracked and their location known at all times + kept in suitable containers to protect against accidental damage or loss + be inspected and tested every two years.
Controlled Waste Regulations 2012	Refuse generated by household and commercial activities contribute to household and commercial waste, while building sites and demolition debris contribute to industrial waste. Local authorities must collect or take the waste to landfills or recycling facilities.
Dangerous Substances and Explosive Atmospheres Regulations (DSEAR) 2002	Protects workers from fire and explosion risks associated with explosive substances, pressurised gases and corrosive substances.
Hazardous Waste Regulations 2005	Hazardous waste is defined as material that contains substances that could be harmful to human health or the environment. Wastes that are considered hazardous include asbestos, chemicals (such as brake fluid and printer toner), batteries, fluorescent tubes and refrigerators.

Dark smoke Produced by the burning of toxic material such as rubber tyres, wet wood and plastics.

121

Environmental considerations

ISO 14001

ISO 14001 is an internationally agreed standard that sets out the requirements for an environmental management system. It helps organisations improve their environmental performance through more efficient use of resources and reduction of waste.

Waste disposal

Benefits and limitations of different methods of waste disposal are shown in Table 12.6.

Table 12.6 Benefits and limitations of different methods of waste disposal

Waste disposal method	Benefits	Limitations
Landfill *Burial of waste material*	A more cost effective alternative to recycling	Extensive land use Groundwater can be contaminated with heavy metal ions Plastics that are not biodegradable may not decompose Toxic chemicals can be produced
Reuse *Make something else from a product*	Reduces single-use items and waste	Products that are reused often have a lower quality
Recycling *Material or product can be reprocessed into something else*	The recycling of materials can be more energy-efficient and carbon-friendly than producing new materials Landfill waste is reduced	Difficulty in separating useful materials from waste A costly investment A certain amount of waste cannot be recycled
Controlled waste *Domestic, commercial, and industrial waste, litter and refuse*	Reducing toxic waste in landfills	A licensed waste disposal facility must be used for the disposal of waste Expensive

Exam tip

Questions may be asked on the methods of waste disposal, so make sure you can remember at least one benefit and one limitation for each method.

Typical mistake

Be sure you understand the difference between the Environmental Protection Act (EPA) and the Clean Air Act (CAA). The EPA advises how to manage and control pollution while the CAA looks only at improving air quality.

Now test yourself

TESTED ○

10 What does the acronym LOTO mean?

11 Which Act covers the height of chimneys?

12 What is ISO 14001?

Summary

In this content area you learned about:
+ the main requirements of key health and safety legislation applicable to engineering activities
+ the importance of health and safety practices within the workplace
+ responsibilities for health and safety
+ health and safety considerations in specific engineering contexts
+ principles and practices relating to environmental legislation and considerations.

Revision activity

Create a mind map that show various methods of waste disposal.

Check your understanding and progress at **www.hoddereducation.co.uk/myrevisionnotes**

1 Name **one** of the main employer requirements of the Management of Health and Safety at Work Regulations (MHSWR). [1]

2 Define the meaning of the acronym RIDDOR. [1]

3 Give the meaning of the abbreviation COSSH. [1]

4 Name one type of notice a HSE inspector can issue. [1]

5 Give **three** responsibilities of employees under HASAWA. [3]

6 State an item of PPE that protects the ears. [1]

7 Describe **two** hazards to which engineers are exposed. [2]

8 Explain the meaning of asphyxiation. [2]

9 Describe the purpose of the Clean Air Act (CAA). [2]

10 Describe why lock out tag out (LOTO) is required. [1]

11 Name the legislation that covers storage of chemicals. [1]

12 Explain a safe system of work. [2]

13 Describe what must be done to minimise risk from manual handling. [1]

14 Describe why there is a need for legislation in the engineering industry. [1]

15 Describe **one** benefit and **one** limitation of reusing waste. [2]

16 Describe **two** ways in which moving parts can cause injury. [2]

17 Describe what is meant by a health and safety culture in the workplace. [2]

18 Describe the three stages of risk assessment. [3]

19 Discuss the benefits to an organisation of implementing ISO 14001. [6]

12 Health and safety principles and coverage

13 Business, commercial and financial awareness

13.1 Principles of commercial operations and markets

Commercial priorities

REVISED

Table 13.1 Commercial priorities

Priority	Description
Profit	All companies seek to make a profit (to make more money than they spend), so they can grow, possibly invest and make more money. Publicly traded companies are legally required to make the most profit they can for their shareholders.
Efficiency	This means making the best use of company **resources** and may include, for example, a reduction in waste, a move towards automation, or the introduction of faster or greener ways of working that aim to reduce cost while producing the same standard of product.
Value added	**Value added** costs are costs which arise from activities which increase the worth of a product. For example, machining a part to the requirements of an engineering drawing or painting a part to the customers' requirements are both 'adding value'.
Non-value added	Non-value added costs are costs which arise from activities that do not add worth to a product, for example, if a part has to be moved from a machine at one end of the factory to a machine at the other end of the factory, or when a product is held in stores waiting to be shipped. These tasks do not add value to the product and so should be minimised wherever possible.
Competition	What are other companies doing in the same market? How is their product different, better, worse or better value than the one produced in your company?
Supply and demand	What is the potential market for the product? If too many products are produced, prices may drop or sales decline. Too few products and prices may remain high, or space for a competitor may be made. Companies must gauge supply and demand for their product and make decisions accordingly.

> **Exam tip**
>
> Always make sure you back up your answer with a reason 'because'. For example, 'This is an example of a direct cost because...'.

> **Revision activity**
>
> Research the manufacture of ballpoint pens and think about the type of manufacturing processes which would be applied. What might some direct and indirect costs be? How would you apply the indirect costs to the price of the pen?

> **Resource** A supply of something (for example, people, stock, money, materials) that can be used to ensure effective functionality.
>
> **Value added** Increase in value of a product after each stage of development and production.

Markets

REVISED

Customers

Who are the customers for a product and where are they based? The customers may be local, somewhere else in the country, or overseas. For each of these types of customer, there will be different expectations and challenges. Transport, culture, currencies, laws and taxes are some of the things to consider. Market research can help to find out what your customer wants or to identify gaps in the market.

Check your understanding and progress at **www.hoddereducation.co.uk/myrevisionnotes**

13.2 Business and commercial practices

Legal practices

Table 13.2 Business practices

Business practice	Description
Tendering	This process involves sending out details of a job or project to several companies with the intention that they bid (or tender) to do the work. This is also referred to as sub-contracting to suppliers.
Contract	An agreement. This can be spoken (harder to enforce) or written; however, in this context it is a legally binding written agreement signed by two people or representatives of companies detailing what will be paid, to whom, what will be delivered, where and when.
Warranty	A guarantee that the product will work for a certain length of time, and details of responsibility and compensation should the product fail.
Force majeure	Unexpected delays and disruptions that prevent a party (supplier) from completing a contract. *Force majeure* is a term that refers to liabilities incurred by the supplier (signatory to the contract) for not completing their job due to unforeseeable circumstances, such as a war, global pandemic or flood.
Indemnity clauses, liability clauses	Sections of a contract which state that a company, supplier or manufacturer will have to pay fines or costs (is 'liable', for example, for extra work or to replace goods) if they fail to meet the initial agreement obligations, for example, if they supply the product late or to an inferior standard.
Resource allocation and planning	The **hierarchy** of a company is determined by its management structure. Managers are employed by companies to oversee the various levels of staff within the business. Management is responsible for deciding where it is best to deploy expertise and people, and where to invest money. A larger workforce, new technology, new markets? How should resources be invested or deployed now, next week, for the next five years?
Training and development	In a rapidly changing work environment, a skilled and trained workforce is an advantage as it means that a company can be more flexible to accommodate changes in customer needs. Companies arrange training for staff to ensure that they are up to date with their business knowledge and also to prove that they value their staff.
Traditional versus agile management	**Traditional business models** have fixed roles and responsibilities. Each step of the traditional project follows the last, and there is a set order (plan, create, review, release). Agile management is a more flexible and iterative approach, where each of these steps can be done at every stage, with the outcomes feeding into the next stage of the process.

> **Hierarchy** The structure of a company or organisation; who is in charge of whom, how departments link to each other.
>
> **Traditional business model** A conventional method of structuring and operating a business, usually involving the linear model of production and sales of goods.

13.3 Financial and economic concepts

Financial responsibility

Financial responsibility

A director of a company has a responsibility to ensure the long term growth of the company; this includes being profitable.

It is also a legal requirement to keep financial records.

This means recording:
+ all money received and spent by the company
+ details of assets owned by the company
+ debts the company owes or is owed

- stock the company owns at the end of the financial year and records of the stocktakings used to calculate the stock figure
- all goods bought and sold and who bought and sold them (unless the company is a retail business)

The records can include receipts, invoices, petty cash books, orders and delivery notes, contracts, sales books and till rolls, bank statements and correspondence. These will be needed for annual accounts and tax return and must be kept for a minimum of six years.

Table 13.3 Financial concepts

Responsibility	Explanation
Source of finance: loans	When a company takes a loan, they borrow money from a bank or another lender and pay the sum back over an extended time period. The repayments include compound interest in addition to the original amount.
Source of finance: shares	A publicly traded company is on a stock market ('floated' on the stock market), allowing others to buy a 'share' of the company. Shareholders profit when the company does well but can also lose money if the company does badly. Floating a business on the stock market can raise money from investors who buy shares in the hope of sharing in the profits of the company.
Source of finance: capital	Business capital is money saved in the business that the company needs in order to function. Sources of capital are personal savings, money invested by friends and family, venture capitalists (VC), corporations, government, or private loans, work or business operations, or from the business being floated on the stock exchange (as this is another method of raising additional funds).
Budget	A detailed forecast of how much money the company has and how much the company expects to spend in the future.
Transaction	The exchange of money when buying and selling.
Costs: indirect	Costs which are not directly related to the manufacture of the product.
Costs: Overheads	Overheads include indirect business costs such as the cost of the teabags in the canteen, the costs of computers used by engineers and office workers and the office electricity bill. These are 'hidden' costs that are essential for the smooth running of the business.
Costs: direct	These are costs that are directly related to the production of the product, such as the cost of the electricity used by the machine producing the product, or the wages of the shop floor workers who operate the machinery that produces the product. These costs are more straightforward to calculate and set against each product.
Payment terms	Questions to consider include: how long until goods have to be paid for or how long until the loan is repaid? What are the interest rates? What happens if payment is missed?
Revenue	How much money is flowing into the company. Gross revenue is the total amount that products are sold for. Net revenue is the gross revenue minus any costs of producing the product.
Creditors and debtors	Debtors are people or companies who owe money to another person or company. For example, as a mobile phone owner on a contract, you are paying for your phone over two years before you become the 'owner'. You are a debtor or borrower from the phone company. The phone company is a creditor. Creditors provide services, products or finance and are owed payment for them.
Cash flow	The balance of money going into and going out of the company. For example, it may be essential that a customer pays on time so that money becomes available to purchase the parts for the next order.
Profit and loss, and breaking even	Being in profit means that more money is made in sales of the product than is spent manufacturing it. When a loss is made, the revenue from a product is less than it costs to produce it. When a company breaks even, they are spending the same amount to manufacture the product as the money being made from product sales.
Assets and liabilities	Assets are tangibles (physical things) that a company owns, such as buildings and machines. Liabilities are things that a company is yet to pay for, for example, a manufacturing machine that has arrived but is not due to be paid for until the end of the month. Until it is paid for on that date, the machine cost is classed as a liability.

Responsibility	Explanation
Assets: depreciation	The amount by which assets (things that are owned) lose their value over time. Depreciation can occur from use of the asset or obsolescence, but is also (in accountancy terms) a way of spreading the cost of the asset over its lifetime. For example, the value of a car reduces over time from the date of its initial purchase. A brand new phone will be worth much less in two years' time.
Solvency	Solvency is the ability of a company to meet its financial obligations. Proving long-term stability is an important part of being solvent; solvency is not just being able to pay bills.
Taxes and rates	Taxes and rates are costs which must be paid to the government, such as car tax, value added tax (VAT) and income tax. Rates are fixed taxes, usually associated with utilities (water or electricity).

Typical mistake

Don't confuse direct and indirect costs. Remember they **both** need to be covered in the cost of the product for the company to make a profit. However, the method in which they are divided up against the cost of the product differs.

Now test yourself

TESTED

1 When might *force majeure* be used?
2 Why do companies need to make a profit?
3 What is the difference between direct and indirect costs?
4 What is the difference between an asset and a liability?
5 What taxes in the UK are applied to manufactured goods?
6 What methods are available to raise capital?
7 Why would you use a written contract instead of a verbal agreement?
8 What is needed for a written contract to be agreed?

Summary

In this content area you learned about:
+ key terms used in business for planning and budgeting
+ an overview of business practices and principles.

Exam-style questions

1 Define efficiency in the context of commercial operations. [1]
2 Explain the concept of supply and demand. [2]
3 Describe two value added operations in an engineering company. [1]
4 Evaluate the role of research and development in developing new products. [4]
5 Define financial responsibility. [1]
6 Discuss the importance of cash flow in an engineering organisation. [3]
7 Evaluate the advantages and disadvantages for three different ways of raising capital and their appropriateness for a small engineering firm. [12]

14 Professional responsibilities, attitudes, and behaviours

14.1 Professional conduct and responsibilities in the workplace

Conduct and responsibilities

Job description

A job description is an account of the job role and the qualities required in the person carrying out that role. This will typically include working hours, skills and personal qualities needed, and details of what the employee will be doing.

Behaviour required in the workplace

Appropriate behaviour is the manner in which employees should conduct themselves. This includes being punctual and having good attendance, a professional appearance, a good attitude to work, working well with colleagues and treating customers and colleagues with respect.

Personal conduct

Reputation

This is the perception that others, such as your colleagues, customers and the public, have of you. Are you known for the quality of your work, are you good at your job, and are you punctual and reliable?

Ethical responsibilities

Professional engineers are governed by an ethical code. This means there are expectations about workplace behaviour and how they should act in order not to bring the profession in disrepute.

Engineers should act with integrity, ensure that that their work is performed with accuracy and rigour, which means they should not cut corners or misrepresent what they have done. An engineer's work should also promote equality, diversity, accessibility and inclusion.

Equality, diversity and inclusion

Under the Equality Act 2010 companies are not allowed to discriminated against based on the following characteristics: age, disability, gender reassignment, marriage and civil partnership, pregnancy and maternity, race, religion or belief, sex and sexual orientation.

All employers must:
+ ensure they do not unfairly discriminate in any aspect of work
+ take steps to prevent and protect people from discrimination
+ look after the wellbeing of their employees

Advice and support

Don't be afraid to ask for help if needed from teachers or colleagues. Professional bodies such as the IEEE or IMechE can also offer support.

Levels of accountability in organisational structures

Table 14.1 Responsibilities and accountabilities of different roles within an engineering company

Role within the organisation	Main responsibilities	Accountable to
Apprentice	Developing their knowledge and skills 'on the job' Completing the relevant qualifications for the job role they are working towards, e.g. machine operator	Line manager Coach/mentor Apprenticeship/training provider
Operator	Safely operating tools, equipment and machinery used to manufacture, test or maintain products	Line/department manager Team leader
Manager	Leading and organising teams or groups of employees Setting targets, e.g. for production Reviewing performance of individual team members	Senior managers Directors
Director	Overall management and oversight of the company and its operations Strategic decision-making	Chief executive officer (CEO) Shareholders External regulators

Revision activity

Research the Equality Act 2010. What are the nine protected characteristics?

14.2 Continuous professional development (CPD) and professional recognition

All professional bodies set professional standards that they expect their members to adhere to. As a member of a professional engineering body (for example, IMechE, IEE or IET), engineers are expected to keep up to date with emerging technology, work practices and qualifications and to keep a record of any CPD they undertake. This development can take various forms, for example training courses, industry placement, academic study, events and seminars.

Professional standards Expectations that are set by the professional bodies which govern skills and behaviours within a profession.

Professional engineering body A recognised engineering organisation. In order to be a Chartered Engineer, you must be registered with a recognised engineering organisation (see further: www.engc.org.uk/about-us/our-partners/professional-engineering-institutions/)

IMechE Institution of Mechanical Engineers.

IEE Institute of Electrical Engineers.

IET Institution of Engineering and Technology.

Revision activity

Research engineering institutions, what they are for and why you might want to become a member.

Exam tip

Ensure that you know the names and abbreviations of all the main engineering bodies.

14.3 Human factors within engineering and manufacturing contexts

Human factors is the study of how people operate within an environment. It is often used in safety-critical environments, for example an aircraft cockpit or a nuclear power station, to create best practice and safety procedures.

129

Typical mistake

Human factors is an often misunderstood and neglected area of the design process. It is a large area of study and there are great benefits if human factors is integrated into the design early in the process.

Table 14.2 Causes of human error and how they can be avoided

Cause of human error	How it can be avoided
Insufficient training	Ensure all workers are suitably qualified for their role.
	Ensure workers are trained in the safe operation of all tools and equipment that they need to use.
	Use standard operating procedures.
	Provide and engage in ongoing CPD.
Fatigue	Ensure appropriate limits on working hours.
	Ensure workers take regular breaks.
	Ensure workers do not operate tools or machinery while tired.
Excessive workload	Plan effectively to ensure workers have enough time to complete tasks allocated to them.
	Allocate tasks, tools, equipment and resources effectively.
	Ensure good teamworking.
Stress	Encourage mental wellbeing within the workplace.
	Make use of flexible hours and remote working, if appropriate.
	Provide opportunities for counselling and mental health support.

Physical and mental characteristics must be considered when designing a safe engineering workplace. The members of a workforce need to be able to function safely and with ease when carrying out their day-to-day roles. When designing products and processes, human factors should also be considered; for example, not putting important warning lights in a user's peripheral vision, or making sure that work stations easily allow for repetitive tasks to be undertaken without the user having to over stretch.

Mistakes made in the workplace can often be attributed to human error. The possibility of human error should be minimised as much as possible. You should be aware of human factors in manufacture and what the causes of errors can be (see Table 14.2).

Physical characteristics
The defining features of the human body.

Mental characteristics
The defining features of a person's mental capabilities – how they work and their approach in the workplace.

Revision activity

Consider the workplace design for a small workshop that produces bird boxes. What health and safety issues might be involved in ensuring the safety of the workforce and efficient productivity?

Now test yourself

TESTED ◯

1 What is ethics and how does it apply to engineering?
2 How might a knowledge of human factors inform your design?
3 What behaviours are expected in the workplace?
4 Give three examples of CPD.

Summary

In this content area you learned about:
+ the role of job descriptions
+ expected workplace behaviours, accountabilities and responsibilities
+ CPD, professional bodies' standards and expectations
+ workplace design and minimising human error.

Exam-style questions

1 Name two engineering institutions. [1]

2 State three things which would be regarded as good practice in the workplace. [1]

3 What are two common causes of human error? [1]

4 Explain the importance of ongoing CPD. [3]

5 Explain what measures you could take to reduce worker fatigue. [2]

6 Evaluate the benefits of belonging to a professional engineering body against the cost of membership. [4]

7 State two potential consequences of bad workplace practice or behaving in an unprofessional manner. [2]

15 Stock and asset management

15.1 Stock and inventory management principles and practices

Stock and inventory principles

REVISED

Demand and turnover

+ Demand is how much stock is required at a particular stage or point in the manufacturing process.
+ Turnover is the rate at which stock is used (or sold) and replaced. Some stock items have a higher turnover than others.

Cost of inventory

Costs associated with storing stock can include:

+ cost of storage space, for example building rent, energy and staffing costs.
+ transporting or moving stock
+ the disposal of stock when it is no longer needed.

Redundant stock, write down and obsolescence

Redundant stock is stock that is no longer needed by a business. For example, if a particular type of product is no longer being produced, the stored materials that are used to make it might become redundant.

A 'write down' takes place when stock nears or reaches the end of its useful lifespan. At this point the value of the stock is either reduced or it is removed from the company's inventory entirely.

Stock becomes obsolete when it becomes outdated, for example, parts or components that are no longer used.

Other stock management considerations

+ The minimum levels at which a company needs to reorder each item of stock.
+ The supply chain for each item of stock required.
+ How the stock will be packaged while it is stored.

Stock and inventory practices

REVISED

For each of the practices used, it is important to plan the material and stock requirements for the different manufacturing processes involved.

> **Demand** How much the stock is required at a particular stage or point in the manufacturing process.
>
> **Turnover** The rate at which stock is used and replaced.
>
> **Redundant stock** Stock that is no longer needed by a business.

> **Revision activity**
>
> Produce a mind map displaying the factors that need to be considered when managing stock within a manufacturing company.

Check your understanding and progress at **www.hoddereducation.co.uk/myrevisionnotes**

Table 15.1 Stock and inventory practices

Practice	What it involves	Advantages	Disadvantages
Just in time (JIT)	Stock is purchased when it is needed, as it is needed	Reduced storage space and costs Prevents over production	Need for flexible suppliers of stock Difficulty in reacting to a sudden increase in demand
Made to stock	Products are produced to meet expected customer demand	Products are ready to be shipped as soon as they are ordered Ease of manufacturing planning	Possibility of 'dead' stock if a company makes too much of a product Increased storage space requirements and costs
Made to order	Products are only manufactured when they are ordered by a customer	No need for a finished product to be sitting around in the factory or stores Cost-efficient and straightforward	Workers can spend a lot of wasted time waiting for orders Staff may become overwhelmed if a large number of orders come in at the same time
Material requirements planning	Systematic scheduling and control of materials needed for production processes	Ensures that materials are available when needed Helps to plan for and deal with shortages or delays in the supply chain	Can take time and resources away from other activities

Exam tip

Make sure you understand and can explain each of the stock and inventory practices, and their advantages and disadvantages.

Now test yourself   TESTED ⦿

1 What does stock become when it is outdated?
2 What procedure takes place when stock nears or reaches the end of its useful lifespan?
3 Which stock and inventory practice involves producing products to meet expected customer demand?

Revision activity

Find examples of products made using each of the stock and inventory practices given in Table 15.1. For each example, explain why the practice was used and how it benefitted the company who manufactured the product.

Just in time (JIT) A stock and inventory practice where stock is purchased when it is needed, as it is needed.

Made to stock A stock and inventory practice where products are produced to meet expected customer demand.

Made to order A stock and inventory practice where products are only manufactured when they are ordered by a customer.

15.2 Asset management and control principles

Engineering companies must keep track of the number and value of their assets, including for example hand tools, machines, computers, desks and chairs.

Assets Resources with economic value that are owned by a company.

Capacity management

✚ Engineering companies need to plan their resource requirements efficiently, to avoid ending up with too much or too little of each resource during the manufacturing process.

✚ It is important to try to avoid bottlenecks or points in the production process that might slow it down, e.g. due to lack of machine capacity or by being short-staffed.

> **Bottleneck** A point in the production process that slows it down.

Key stages of asset life-cycle management

There are four key stages in the management of asset life cycles:

✚ planning the assets required
✚ acquisition of the assets
✚ operation and maintenance of the assets
✚ disposal of the assets in line with procedures and regulations.

Budgetary control practices

✚ The entire life cycle of stock and assets must be considered, for example when designing products, planning, ordering and receiving stock, producing products, packaging and dispatching products, and disposing of waste.

✚ The life cycle should be considered in the context of the whole life of the product being produced.

✚ Depreciation must also be considered. This is the reduction in value of an asset over time, for example due to wear and tear, or obsolescence. For example, a new car depreciates in value the moment it is driven off the forecourt.

> **Life cycle** Consideration of the different stages in the life of an asset.
>
> **Depreciation** The reduction value of an asset over time.

Now test yourself

4 Give two examples of bottlenecks in manufacturing.
5 What are the first two key stages of the asset life cycle?
6 Give one example of a cause of depreciation of an asset.

Typical mistake

It is easy to confuse stock and assets. Make sure you understand the differences between them, and the practices used to manage and control them.

Summary

In this content area you learned about:
✚ the different considerations when managing stock
✚ the different stock and inventory management practices used by engineering companies
✚ the purpose of effective asset management and how it is achieved
✚ the key stages of asset life cycle management
✚ the budgetary and control practices used by engineering companies.

Revision activity

Summarise the life cycle of an asset, such as a particular piece of equipment or a machine. What are the key considerations at each stage? Illustrate your findings in an annotated flowchart.

Exam-style questions

1 Explain why engineering companies need to plan their resources efficiently. [3]
2 Give three examples of assets that would typically be owned by an engineering company. [3]
3 Explain why disposal must be considered as part of asset life cycle management. [2]
4 Define the term 'depreciation'. [1]
5 Explain how a forklift truck owned by a company would depreciate over time. [4]

16 Continuous improvement

16.1 Continuous improvement principles and practices

Engineering businesses need to continually improve their processes, practices and procedures in order to stay competitive. There are different strategies they can use to help them achieve this.

Improving processes

REVISED

+ The first step is reflecting on and evaluating the processes undertaken by the company. This involves looking at what has gone well and identifying any improvements that could be made.
+ Incremental improvements are small, regular changes that, over time, move the business forward.
+ Key performance indicators (KPIs) are measures of how well a company is operating, for example machine changeover time, capacity utilisation or on-time delivery percentage.

> **Key performance indicators (KPIs)**
> Measures of how well a company is operating.

Implementation

REVISED

The PDCA cycle (plan, do, check, act) is a way of implementing and managing change (see Figure 16.1). It is a cyclical, iterative process:
+ **plan** – identify the improvements required and how they will be achieved
+ **do** – implement the planned improvement activity
+ **check** – compare performance against the expected results
+ **act** – correct any errors identified.

> **PDCA cycle** A way of implementing and managing change (plan, do, check, act).

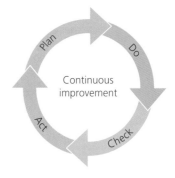

Figure 16.1 PDCA cycle

Eight wastes

REVISED

Table 16.1 The eight wastes

Name of waste	Description
Transportation	Unnecessary movement of materials and products
Inventory	Having materials and products that are not currently being processed
Motion	Any movement of people or products that do not add value to what is being produced
Waiting	Time spent waiting for other processes to be carried out
Excess or over production	Producing too many products for the customer demand
Over-processing	Making products to a higher specification than needed, but in the quantities required
Defects	Products that have faults or imperfections, or services that do not meet customer expectations
Skills (unused talent)	poor use of the skills and knowledge available in the workforce

> **Eight wastes** A group of eight potential wastes within a business.

Business improvement strategies

✚ Lean manufacturing is a strategy that aims to reduce the waste from manufacturing and production processes to its absolute minimum (zero waste).

✚ Kaizen is a strategy based around the idea that small, ongoing improvements add up to significant improvements over time. It involves all employees and all processes within a company. Kaizen originated in Japan after WWII.

> **Lean manufacturing** A strategy that aims to reduce the waste from manufacturing and production processes to its absolute minimum.
>
> **Kaizen** A strategy based around the idea that small, ongoing improvements add up to significant improvements over time.

Continuous improvement practices

✚ Value stream mapping (VSM) is used to analyse how materials and information flow through a company by 'walking' the process. It often requires a large investment of time and money.

✚ Visual management involves the use of visual tools to communicate information, thus increasing ease of understanding, aiding productivity and focus and providing risk prevention measures. These could include: shadow boards, progress or countdown boards, traffic lights, health and safety signs and floor markings around machinery. One potential limitation is outdated information if the system is not updated regularly enough.

✚ Six S is an approach to workplace organisation that reduces waste and improves efficiency (see Table 16.2).

Table 16.2 The Six S steps

Name of step	Description
Sort	Identification of the items that are required in the workspace
Set in order	Putting items in the best place for when they are needed
Shine	Cleaning the workplace
Standardise	Establishing procedures to ensure that the first three Ss are maintained
Sustain	Ensuring that the good practices are properly maintained
Safety	Management and minimisation of hazards and risks

✚ Single minute exchange of dies (SMED) is an activity undertaken to reduce changeover times when making a product, e.g. when swapping tools or resetting machine parameters.

✚ Operation effective efficiency (OEE) involves measuring the percentage of planned production time that is actually productive:

$$OEE = \frac{\text{total number of good products produced} \times \text{ideal processing time}}{\text{planned production time}} \times 100$$

✚ Total productive maintenance (TPM) aims to involve the entire workforce in the maintenance of tools and equipment, rather than just a dedicated maintenance team. This reduces downtime and, hence, increases efficiency. It can, however, be time consuming and challenging to implement.

✚ Kanban involves the use of a card system (or a Kanban board) that manages the flow of work within a manufacturing environment. This gives workers clear visual instructions that are easy to follow.

> **Value stream mapping (VSM)** Used to analyse how materials and information flow through a company by 'walking' the process.
>
> **Visual management** The use of visual tools to communicate information, such as shadow boards and traffic lights.
>
> **Six S** An approach to workplace organisation that reduces waste and improves efficiency.
>
> **Single minute exchange of dies (SMED)** A term first used by Toyota. The goal of SMED is to complete every changeover between products in less than a minute.
>
> **Total productive maintenance (TPM)** A strategy that involves all workers in maintenance activities.
>
> **Kanban** The use of a card system (or a Kanban board) to manage the flow of work within a manufacturing environment.

Table 16.3 Value stream mapping

Step number	Activity	Value added?	Type of waste
1	Move pallet from stores to work area	No	Transportation
2	Pallet in work-in-progress area	No	Waiting (time)
3	Move pallet to machine	No	Transportation
4	Load part into machine by hand	No	Transportation
5	Machine drill three holes	Yes	N/A

Now test yourself

TESTED ⬤

1 What are KPIs?

2 What are incremental improvements?

3 Name the eight wastes.

4 Which continuous improvement practice is used to analyse how materials and information flow through a company via 'walking' the process?

5 What does SMED stand for?

6 How is OEE calculated?

7 Which continuous improvement practice aims to involve the entire workforce in the maintenance of tools and equipment?

8 Which continuous improvement practice can involve the use of a card system that manages the flow of work within a manufacturing environment?

Exam tip

Make sure you understand the purpose, methodology, benefits and limitations of the different continuous improvement practices.

Typical mistake

The benefits of the different improvement practices are often misunderstood or mixed up. Make sure you know the purpose of each one.

Revision activity

Use the internet to research two different companies that use continuous improvement strategies and practices within their workplace. For each, describe the methodologies involved and explain the benefits to the company.

Summary

In this content area you learned about:

+ the main stages of the PDCA cycle
+ the purpose and use of KPIs
+ how the eight wastes affect the performance of engineering activities
+ the purpose of Lean and Kaizen techniques
+ the purpose and benefits of different continuous improvement practices.

Exam-style questions

1 One of the eight wastes is 'excess production'. Describe **two** examples of how this affects the performance of a manufacturing company. [4]

2 State the steps of the PDCA cycle. [4]

3 Give **three** examples of key performance indicators (KPIs) for an engineering business. [3]

4 Explain one benefit of visual management to an engineering company. [2]

5 Give **two** benefits of TPM to an engineering company. [2]

6 State the purpose of SMED. [1]

7 A company mass produces car parts. They have decided to implement Kanban in their factory. Explain **two** benefits of this to the company. [4]

17 Project and programme management

17.1 Principles of project management

Project brief, goals and success criteria

For any project:
+ the project brief is a short summary of the problem to be solved
+ project goals are the desired outcomes of the project
+ success criteria are a list of requirements that the project will be judged against.

> **Project brief** A short summary of the problem to be solved.

Project life cycle

A typical project follows the following life cycle:
+ initiation – this is where the project is identified, defined and approved
+ planning – in this stage the timescales and resources required are identified
+ implementation – the plan is put into action and the project is undertaken
+ monitoring – this is where the progress of the project is checked against the plan and desired outcomes
+ reporting – those involved in the project report progress and any problems faced
+ evaluation – the success of the project is evaluated against the original criteria and improvements are identified for future projects.

> **(Project) life cycle** The different stages that a project follows.

Constraints

These are the limitations on a project, for example, available time and resources, costs and budgets, and specific client requirements.

Risk management

During a project there are several risks that could affect its success. These must be managed throughout the project life cycle. Typical examples include:
+ the budget and costs associated with the project
+ the quality of processes and outcomes
+ health and safety hazards, requirements and regulations
+ the availability of equipment and resources (this includes staff and materials)
+ communication between team members and stakeholders
+ potential damage to company reputation
+ changing client or customer requirements.

> **Risk management** Management of the risks that could affect the success of a project.

Collaborative working

Benefits of collaborative working include:
+ sharing of different skills, knowledge and expertise
+ increased involvement and feedback from stakeholders, including clients
+ improved problem solving – when working as a team, there is a greater pool of knowledge to draw from for answers to problems that can arise.

> **Collaborative working** Working together with other engineers and stakeholders.

Limitations of collaborative working include:
+ the time needed to consult different stakeholders
+ differences of opinion can cause conflict within a group
+ lack of overall focus – projects can become 'bloated' with too many ideas.

Matrix working

This is a collaborative working structure where employees report to a variety of managers. For example, they may report to a manager related to their function, but also a specific project or product manager, or even a regional manager if applicable.

Collaborative technologies

Technologies such as email, instant messaging and video conferencing software can be used to assist with collaborative working when people are not based in the same location.

Now test yourself   TESTED ⬤

1   List the first two stages of the project life cycle.

2   State what is meant by project constraints.

3   Give two benefits of collaborative working.

4   What is a short summary of the project to be completed called?

5   What are the desired outcomes of a project called?

> **Matrix working** A collaborative working style where employees report to a variety of managers.

> **Exam tip**
>
> Make sure you can explain the benefits and limitations of collaborative working and give examples of its use.

> **Revision activity**
>
> For an engineering project you are about to complete, identify the possible risks associated with it and explain how you will manage them. You could present your response as a spider chart or mind map.

17.2 Roles and responsibilities in projects

Table 17.1 Roles and responsibilities within projects

Role	Responsibilities within a project
Stakeholder – client	Initiates the project and agrees a project brief with the team
	Sets out their needs and wants for the project
Stakeholder – regulators	Check that work complies with regulatory requirements, e.g. the Health and Safety Executive may inspect the workplace if safety concerns are raised
	Can issue penalties (e.g. compliance notices, fines or prosecution) where compliance does not occur
Project manager	Has overall responsibility for the success of the project
	Manages the budget, resources and staff involved
	Monitors progress throughout the project against the project plan
Team members	Complete different aspects of the project according to their skills, knowledge and function within the team
	Collaborate with other team members
	Communicate by reporting progress and issues to the project manager

> **Stakeholders** People with a vested interest or 'stake' in the success of a project.
>
> **Project manager** Has overall responsibility for the success of a project.

6   Give two examples of stakeholders in a project.

7   State three responsibilities of a project manager.

8   State the role that is responsible for completing the bulk of the work within a project.

9   Who can issue fines to a company if they do not comply with relevant legislation?

10 Who usually initiates a project?

Revision activity

A team is responsible for manufacturing the wings for a bespoke light aircraft. Identify the different roles and responsibilities of the people involved in this project.

17.3 Project planning and control

Resource requirements   REVISED ⬤

A project plan needs to consider the following resource requirements:

+ the time needed to complete each stage of the project and the project as whole
+ the budget for the project and how this will spent
+ the human resources required, i.e. staffing and personnel availability
+ how information at each stage of the project will be communicated, for example by face-to-face, written or online methods
+ the facilities required for the production and manufacturing tasks
+ training of staff – if this is required, then any associated costs should be added to the project budget.

Planning techniques   REVISED ⬤

Table 17.2 Planning techniques

Planning technique	Description
Gantt charts	Give a graphical representation of the project tasks that need to be completed over time. The time taken to complete each task is included, as well as the required resources (see Figure 17.2).
Critical path analysis (CPA)	This is used to determine the minimum time necessary to complete the project.
Project evaluation review technique (PERT) chart	The **management of interdependencies** – where each project task is shown as a shape (within the overall chart) along with the estimated time needed to complete it. The tasks are linked together in dependencies. For example, if task 1 must be completed before task 2 starts, then task 2 is dependent on task 1 (see Figure 17.3).
Contingency planning	When an alternative 'plan B' is put in place in case problems faced during the project prevent the original plan from being executed.

Gantt chart A planning chart that gives a graphical representation of the project tasks that need to be completed over time.

Critical path analysis (CPA) An analysis technique used to determine the minimum time necessary to complete a project.

Project evaluation review technique (PERT) chart A chart displaying each project task as a shape and the estimated time needed to complete it.

Management of interdependencies Where each project task is shown as a shape in a PERT chart, along with the estimated time needed to complete it.

Contingency planning When a 'plan B' is put in place in case problems faced during the project prevent the original plan from being executed.

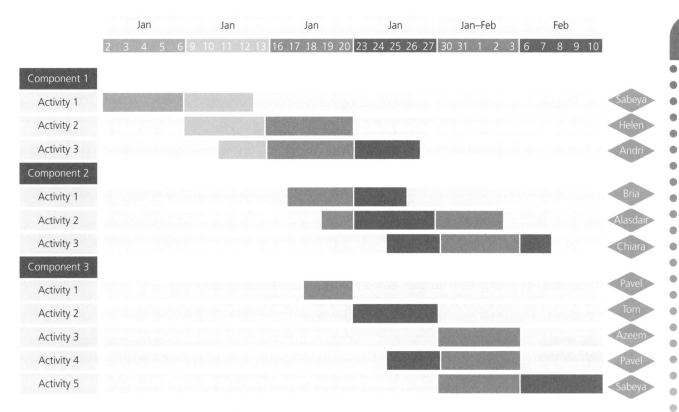

Figure 17.1 An example of a Gantt chart

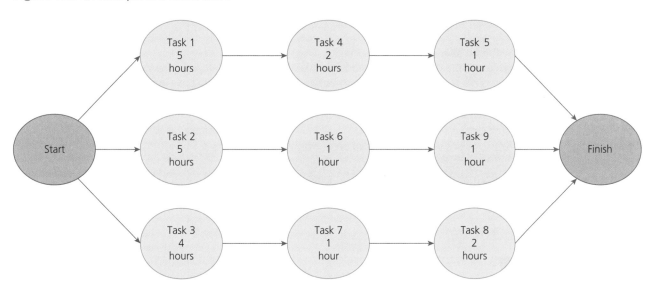

Figure 17.2 An example of a PERT chart

Project control

REVISED ⬤

It is important to monitor a project as it progresses. If problems are identified, these can be dealt with quickly and effectively. Regular reports should be submitted to the project manager, giving information about the project's progress against the budget, any costs incurred, quality of outcomes and time taken.

Management approaches

Table 17.3 Management approaches

Management approach	Description
Manage by stages approach	Where the manager makes checks at defined set points during the implementation of the plan. This allows the project to be overseen as a series of manageable chunks, but it can lack flexibility.
Manage by exception approach	Where reports or checks are only made at stages where there is deviation from the norm, such as a quality issue. This saves the time of managers but is corrective rather than preventative.

Manage by stages A management control technique where the manager makes checks at defined set points.

Manage by exception A management control technique where checks are only made at stages where there is deviation from the norm.

Review and evaluation of completed projects

Once a project has been completed, implemented processes can be reviewed and analysed so that lessons are learnt for the future. What approach was successful and what could be done better next time around?

Typical mistake

Managing by stages and managing by exception are two different project management approaches, but it is easy to mix them up. Make sure you understand both approaches and how projects are managed using them.

Summary

In this content area you learned about:
+ the ways in which projects are defined and structured in terms of their goals and success criteria
+ the different stages of the project life cycle
+ the types of risk within a project that must be managed
+ the benefits and limitations of collaborative working
+ the main roles and responsibilities within projects and how they contribute to its success
+ the resource requirements that should be considered in a project plan
+ the methods and techniques used in project planning
+ the approaches used to manage and control projects
+ the benefits of reviewing how well a project went.

Now test yourself

11 Budget and time are two examples of resources that should be considered in a project plan. Name three other examples of resources that should be considered.

12 Explain the purpose of critical path analysis (CPA).

13 What does PERT stand for?

14 What is put in place in case problems prevent the original plan for a project from being executed?

TESTED

Revision activity

Research the different approaches to project management and control. When and how might each be used? Present your results as a table.

Exam-style questions

1 Explain the purpose of a project brief. [2]

2 What are 'project goals'? [1]

3 Describe the final stage of the project life cycle. [2]

4 Explain the purpose of monitoring in the product life cycle. [2]

5 An engineering team is working collaboratively across several different countries. Give **three** examples of technologies that could assist with this. [3]

6 Explain the purpose of industry regulators. [2]

7 Explain the responsibilities of a client within an engineering project. [3]

8 Define the term 'human resources' as related to a project plan. [1]

9 Describe what is meant by a project budget. [2]

10 Describe a PERT chart. [3]

11 Explain the difference between management by stages and management by exception. [2]

12 Give one benefit and one limitation of management by exception. [2]

Glossary

Accuracy How close a measurement is to a known standard. Page 61

Actuator A device that converts electrical, electronic or mechanical signals into physical movement. Page 92

Aerodynamics The study of how objects move through the air. Page 66

Ageing A process caused by gradual degradation processes combined over a long time. Page 76

Algebra Uses letters to represent the variables in an equation. Page 37

Alloy A material that is formed by combining two or more metals. Page 71

Amorphous structure A non-crystalline structure that does not follow an organised lattice arrangement. Page 73

Analogue signals Continuous signals that can take any value within a given range. Page 88

Anthropometric data Values relating to people across a wide range of sizes and abilities, for example the height and reach of the population. Page 11

Arithmetic progression Sequence of numbers that takes the general form:
$$a_n = a + (n-1)d$$ Page 43

Asphyxiation Process of being deprived of oxygen, which can result in unconsciousness or death; suffocation. Page 119

Assets Resources with economic value that are owned by a company. Page 133

Atom The smallest unit into which matter can be divided without the release of charged particles. Page 62

BIDMAS Defines the order in which to carry out calculations. Page 35

Binary numbers Numbers expressed using base 2. Page 55

Biomass Combustible renewable energy sources including wood, plants and other organic matter. Page 19

Biometric Body measurements and calculations related to human characteristics. Page 25

Bottleneck A point in the production process that slows it down. Page 134

Calculus A branch of mathematics that deals primarily with rates of change. Page 45

Capacitance The ability of a component to store charge, measured in farads (F). Page 85

Cartesian coordinates A system that is used to specify the distances of a point from the coordinate axes on a graph. Page 60

Casting A process that involves pouring molten metal into a mould which cools and solidifies into a desired shape. Page 74

Chatbots (or chatterbot) A software application used to conduct an online chat conversation via text or text-to-speech. Page 22

Circuit protection systems Safety systems that protect circuits from damage in the event of unusual conditions, such as too much voltage or current. Page 87

Coating The addition of a protective layer to prevent damage and corrosion. Page 74

Collaborative working Working together with other engineers and stakeholders. Page 138

Compliance Being in accordance with commands, rules or requests. Page 101

Composites Materials comprising a combination of distinctly different materials that work together to provide improved mechanical properties. Page 71

Compressive strength The ability of material to resist compressive/pushing stresses. Page 70

Concurrent forces Forces where the lines of action all meet at the same point. Page 79

Conduction The transfer of heat through the direct contact of objects. Page 66

Contingency planning When a 'plan B' is put in place in case problems faced during the project prevent the original plan from being executed. Page 140

Convection The transfer of heat through movement of particles in liquids or gases. Page 66

Co-planar forces Forces that are all acting in the same plane. Page 79

Corrosion A chemical process that attacks and consumes a material and degrades its mechanical properties. Page 76

Corrosion resistance The ability of a material to resist the processes that cause corrosion. Page 69

Covalent bonds Bonds that occur when non-metal atoms share a pair of electrons. Page 72

Critical path analysis (CPA) An analysis technique used to determine the minimum time necessary to complete a project. Page 140

Cross (or vector) product Cross or (vector) product of two vectors gives a vector perpendicular to the other two in three-dimensional space. Page 53

Crystalline structure A structure where the molecules are arranged in an ordered, well-defined lattice arrangement. Page 73

Cumulative frequency Running total of the frequencies seen in a frequency distribution. Page 54

Current A flow of electrons, measured in amps (A). Can be direct (DC) or alternating (AC). Page 84

D'Alembert's principle States that the force plus the negative of the mass multiplied by the acceleration is equal to zero, that is, $F - ma = 0$. Page 81

Dark smoke Produced by the burning of toxic material such as rubber tyres, wet wood and plastics. Page 121

Datum A face or edge or other feature from where all the measurements are taken. Page 33

Decimal number Numbers expressed using base 10. Page 55

Decimal numbers Fraction expressed as a number of tenths, hundredths, thousandths etc. stated after a decimal point. Page 35

Decimal places (d.p.) Specifies the required number of digits after the decimal point. Page 36

Demand How much the stock is required at a particular stage or point in the manufacturing process. Page 132

Density The mass of material per unit volume, represented by the symbol ρ. Page 69

Depreciation The reduction value of an asset over time. Page 134

Detail drawing is the name of the type of drawing. A detail drawing shows all the information needed for manufacture. Page 12

Detection The action of identifying something which may be hidden. Page 103

Differentiation Can be used to calculate instantaneous rates of change of a function. Page 47

Digital signals Discrete signals that are either 1 (high) or 0 (low). Page 88

DMAIC A data-driven problem-solving method to help identify and fix problems within a process and improve future output. Page 104

Dot (or scalar) product Dot (or scalar) product of two vectors gives a scalar quantity and can be thought of as directional multiplication. Page 52

Ductility A material's ability to be drawn or stretched without breaking. Page 70

Duty holder A person who is legally responsible. Page 111

Eight wastes A group of eight potential wastes within a business. Page 135

Electrical energy The capacity for an electrical circuit to do work. Page 84

Electrical force The attractive or repulsive interaction between two charged objects. Page 84

Electrical network An arrangement of connected electrical or electronic components. Page 85

Electrical power The rate at which electrical energy is transferred. Page 84

Electrolysis The use of electricity to break down ionic compounds. Page 63

Electromagnetic induction The production of a voltage when a magnet moves within a coil of wire. Page 85

Electrons Negatively charged particles. Page 62

Factorising This involves the extraction of common factors and can be thought of as the opposite of multiplying out. Page 37

Feedback When the output signal from a system becomes an input signal to the same system. Page 97

Ferrous Metals that contain iron e.g. steel. Page 19

Fibre optics Technology that transmits information as light pulses along a glass or plastic fibre. Page 19

Fluid power components The different parts that are connected together to form a fluid power system. Page 94

Fluorescent lighting A low-pressure mercury-vapour gas-discharge lamp that uses fluorescence to produce visible light. Page 22

Fractions Used to express proportions of a whole. Page 36

Fracture When a material separates into two or more parts due to the disconnection of its atomic or molecular bonds. Page 76

Friction Force that acts in opposition to an object moving along a surface. Page 81

Gantt chart A planning chart that gives a graphical representation of the project tasks that need to be completed over time. Page 140

Gear A toothed wheel that is linked together with others to transmit drive. Page 90

Geometric progression Sequence of numbers that takes the general form: $a_n = ar^{n-1}$ Page 44

Gravitational force Force that attracts all objects with mass towards each other. Page 81

Hardness The ability of material to resist indentations, scratches and abrasions. Page 70

Hazard Anything that has the potential to cause harm. Page 111

Heat treatment Processes that use heat in different ways to alter the properties and microstructure of metals. Page 75

Hexadecimal numbers Numbers expressed using base 16. Page 55

Hierarchical Ranked in order of importance. Page 108

Check your understanding and progress at **www.hoddereducation.co.uk/myrevisionnotes**

Hierarchy The structure of a company or organisation, who is in charge of whom, how departments link to each other. Page 125

Histogram A graphical chart that displays data using bars of different height. It groups the data into ranges and the height of each bar shows how many are in each range. Page 105

Hooke's law Law that states that elongation is directly proportional to load. Page 78

Hydraulic system A fluid power system that uses a liquid as the power transmission medium. Page 94

Hydrocarbon gas liquids Liquids made from natural gas and crude oil. Page 19

Hydro-electric power A renewable source of energy that generates power by using a dam to alter the natural flow of a river or other body of water. Page 22

Hydrostatic pressure The pressure exerted by water or liquid on a surface. Page 65

Hypothesis A testable statement of the expected outcome of a study. Page 60

IEE Institute of Electrical Engineers. Page 129

IET Institution of Engineering and Technology. Page 129

IMechE Institution of Mechanical Engineers. Page 129

Imperial (units) Units that are part of the imperial system. Page 59

Indices Powers indicating the number of times a number or variable is multiplied by itself. Page 42

Induction motor An alternating-current motor. Page 22

Inductors Components that use a coil of wire to store energy in the form of a magnetic field. Page 87

Injection moulding Molten thermoplastic is injected into a mould, cooled and solidified into a product. Page 74

Input A device that takes a signal from the environment and turns it into a signal that can be understood by a process device. Page 96

Integers Whole numbers. Page 35

Integration The reverse of differentiation. Page 48

Ionic bonds Bonds that occur between a metal and a non-metal, due to the strong electrostatic forces between positively and negatively charged ions. Page 72

Iteration A further hypothesis if the results of the initial hypothesis are not proven. Page 61

Iterative To take the output from a process, evaluate the results and use this information to improve the process/design. Page 11

Izod test A method of testing the toughness of a material by raising and releasing a pivoting arm to hit the material. Page 77

Just in time (JIT) A stock and inventory practice where stock is purchased when it is needed, as it is needed. Page 133

Kaizen A strategy based around the idea that small, ongoing improvements add up to significant improvements over time. Page 136

Kanban The use of a card system (or a Kanban board) to track production within a manufacturing environment. Page 136

Key performance indicators (KPIs) Measures of how well a company is operating. Page 135

Kinetic energy Energy that an object possesses because of its motion. Page 81

Laminar flow Smooth fluid flow that occurs in parallel layers with no mixing. Page 65

Latent heat Heat added to or removed from a substance that does not cause a change in its temperature but does cause a change in its state, for example from solid to liquid. Page 67

Lean manufacturing A strategy that aims to reduce the waste from manufacturing and production processes to its absolute minimum. Page 136

Legislation A law or set of laws passed by Parliament. Page 101

Life cycle Consideration of the different stages in the life of an asset. Page 134

Lifting operation An operation concerned with the lifting or lowering of a load. Page 112

Light-emitting diodes (LEDs) A semiconductor device that emits light when current flows through it. Page 22

Linear equations These have the standard form $y = mx + c$. Page 38

Linear motion Motion in a straight line. Page 64

Logarithms (logs) Represent the power to which a given base must be raised to represent a given number and are often used when solving problems involving indices. Page 42

Made to order A stock and inventory practice where products are only manufactured when they are ordered by a customer. Page 133

Made to stock A stock and inventory practice where products are produced to meet expected customer demand. Page 133

Magnetic flux density The amount of magnetic flux that passes through a given area at right angles to the magnetic field. Page 85

Maintenance To keep something in good working order and repair. Page 13

Manage by exception A management control technique where checks are only made at stages where there is deviation from the norm. Page 142

Manage by stages A management control technique where the manager makes checks at defined set points. Page 142

Management of interdependencies Where each project task is shown as a shape in a PERT chart, along with the estimated time needed to complete it. Page 140

Material Safety Data Sheet (MSDS) An important information source to help eliminate or reduce the risks associated with hazardous chemicals and substances. Page 116

Matrices Square or rectangular arrays of numbers commonly used to represent vectors or systems of simultaneous equations. Page 53

Matrix working A collaborative working style where employees report to a variety of managers. Page 139

Mean $\bar{x}$ Arithmetic average of the numbers in a data set. Page 54

Mechanical work The amount of energy that is transferred by a force. Page 81

Median Central value in a data set arranged in order of increasing size. Page 54

Mental characteristics The defining features of a person's mental capabilities – how they work and their approach in the workplace. Page 130

Metallic bond The force of attraction between free moving electrons and positive metal ions. Page 72

Metallurgical Relating to the scientific study of the structures and uses of metals. Page 19

Microcontroller A small computer on a chip that is programmed to perform different functions. Page 92

Micrometers Very accurate measurement devices that come in different forms depending on the measurements being taken – inside, outside and depth. Page 62

Mode Value that appears most frequently in a data set. Page 54

Modular PLCs PLCs that have different parts, or modules, that are connected together to form a customisable device. Page 93

Motor A device that creates rotary motion when current flows through it. Page 92

Motor driver An IC that is used to ensure that the motors have the correct current to function. Page 93

Multiples The factors used to create larger forms of SI units. Page 58

Newton's laws of motion Three laws that describe the relationship between the motion of objects and the forces acting on them. Page 79

Non-ferrous Metals that contain no iron e.g. copper. Page 19

N-type semiconductors Semiconductors that have electrons as the majority charge carriers. Page 87

Ohm's law A law that gives the relationship between voltage, current and resistance. Page 86

Orthographic This refers to the style of drawing used by engineers to communicate complex designs. Two-dimensional views of the different surfaces are laid out in line with each other. Page 26

Oscillating motion Motion that moves back and forth about a pivot. Page 64

Output A device that takes the signal from a process device and turns it back into an environmental signal. Page 96

Parallel circuit A circuit arrangement where the components are connected in branches or loops. Page 86

PDCA cycle A way of implementing and managing change (plan, do, check, act). Page 135

Percentages (%) Used to express proportions of a whole as parts per hundred. Page 36

Personal protective equipment (PPE) Clothing or equipment designed to protect a user from workplace hazards. Page 112

Pharmaceuticals Compounds manufactured for use as a medicinal drug. Page 19

Phasor diagram A diagram that shows the phase relationships between two or more alternating quantities in terms of their magnitude and direction. Page 87

Photovoltaic The conversion of light into electricity using semiconducting materials. Page 25

Physical characteristics The defining features of the human body. Page 130

Pneumatic Operated by air or gas under pressure. Page 19

Pneumatic system A fluid power system that uses compressed air as the power transmission medium. Page 94

Point load A load that is applied at a single point on a beam. Page 80

Polar coordinates A system that is used to determine the location of a point on a plane in terms of the distance from a reference point (r) and the angle from a reference direction (θ). Page 60

Potential energy Energy that is stored by an object due to its position. Page 81

Power The rate at which energy is transferred or converted. Page 81

Power series Infinite series of the form:

$$\sum_{n=0}^{\infty} a_n (x-c)^n = a_0 + a_1 (x-c) + a_2 (x-c)^2 + \dots$$

Page 44

Preventative To stop problems which might happen if nothing was done from occurring. Page 13

Probability Used to measure the likelihood that an event will occur. Page 54

Process A device that responds to input signals and alters them in some way. Page 96

Professional engineering body A recognised engineering organisation. In order to be a Chartered Engineer, you must be registered with a recognised Engineering organisation (see further: www.engc.org.uk/about-us/our-partners/professional-engineering-institutions/) Page 129

Professional standards Expectations that are set by the professional bodies that govern skills and behaviours within a profession. Page 129

Programmable logic controller (PLC) A programmable device used to control manufacturing and production processes. Page 93

Project brief A short summary of the problem to be solved. Page 138

Project evaluation review technique (PERT) chart A chart displaying each project task as a shape and the estimated time needed to complete it. Page 140

(Project) life cycle The different stages that a project follows during its life. Page 138

Protons Positively charged particles. Page 62

P-type semiconductors Semiconductors that have holes as the majority charge carriers. Page 87

Pulley A mechanism made using wheels, an axle and a rope, that enables loads to be lifted with less effort. Page 91

Quadratic equations Have the standard form: $y = ax^2 + bx + c$. Page 40

Qualitative data Research about things which can be described. What do users think? Does the product look attractive, is it easy to use? Page 12

Quantitative data Research about things which can be measured in numbers. How fast, tall, heavy, expensive? Page 12

Radians (rad) Unit of measure for angles commonly used in mathematics (2π rad $= 360°$). Page 49

Radiation The transfer of heat via electromagnetic waves. Page 66

Range Difference between the highest and lowest number in a data set. Page 54

Ratios Used to express the relationship between two or more quantities. Page 36

Reciprocating motion Motion that moves back and forth in a straight line. Page 64

Recyclability How suitable a material is for recycling. Page 69

Redundant stock Stock that is no longer needed by a business. Page 132

Renewable power sources Power sources that come from resources that are naturally replenished and sustainable. Page 82

Resistance The opposition to the flow of current, measured in ohms (Ω). Page 84

Resource A supply of something (for example, people, stock, money, materials) that can be used to ensure effective functionality. Page 124

Risk assessment Method of identifying and evaluating hazards to determine whether control measures are sufficient to prevent harm. Page 112

Risk management Management of the risks that could affect the success of a project. Page 138

Rolling A process whereby metal is passed through two rotating rollers, which shapes the metal into a long, thin layer. Page 74

Rotary motion Circular motion. Page 64

Sacrificial anode A metal that is more likely to corrode than the material that is to be protected. Page 76

Sampling The process of selecting batches of products to test. Page 104

Scalar Quantity defined by its magnitude. Page 53

Scale Ratio that is used to express the difference in size between two quantities. Page 36

Scientific method A set series of steps that provide a systematic and objective approach to acquiring knowledge. Page 60

Sensor A component that converts signals from the physical environment into an electrical or electronic signal. Page 92

Sensors Devices that detect changes in the environment around them. Page 99

Sensory stimuli Any event or object that is received by the senses and elicits a response from a person. Page 25

Series circuit A circuit arrangement where components are connected in a line. Page 86

Significant figures (s.f.) Specifies the required number of digits not including any leading zeroes. Page 36

SI (metric) units Units that are part of an agreed international standard for measuring. Page 58

Simplifying equations Making them easier to deal with; involves multiplying out, collecting like terms, and identifying common factors so that an equation can be stated using as few terms as possible. Page 37

Simply supported beams Beams that are resting on two supports and free to move horizontally. Page 80

Simultaneous equations Two or more equations that use the same variables and share at least one set of common solutions. Page 38

My Revision Notes: Engineering and Manufacturing T Level

Single minute exchange of dies (SMED) A term first used by Toyota. The goal of SMED is to complete every changeover between products in less than a minute. Page 136

Six S An approach to workplace organisation that reduces waste and improves efficiency. Page 136

Six Sigma A set of quality management techniques that aim to improve the processes within an organisation to greatly reduce the amount of manufacturing errors and product defects. Page 106

Smart materials Materials that have properties that react in response to an external stimulus, e.g. temperature or light. Page 72

Solutions Homogenous mixtures formed by combining two or more substances. Page 63

Specification A document that states how the component must perform, e.g. maximum size, material, cost. Page 16

Specification limits The values that define whether a product works or not. They assess how capable a process is of meeting the customer requirements. Page 104

Spontaneous combustion A substance unexpectedly bursts into flame without apparent cause. Page 119

Standard deviation Measure of variation about the mean that indicates how widely spread out the values in a data set are. Page 54

Standard form Notation used to express extremely large or extremely small numbers using a suffix in the form $\times 10^{x}$. Page 35

Standardised incidence ratio (SIR) An estimate of the number of cases in a given population compared to what might be 'expected' based on a comparison with the experience in a larger population. Page 113

Subject of an equation The unknown variable being calculated; appears on its own on one side of an equation. Page 37

Submultiples The factors used to create smaller forms of SI units. Page 58

Summing point Produces the algebraic sum of the reference signal and the feedback. Page 97

Supervisory control and data acquisition (SCADA) A PLC-based system that is used to monitor and control industrial engineering processes. Page 93

Surface treatment A process applied to the surface of a material to give it additional wear and corrosion resistance, and/or for aesthetic reasons. Page 75

Sustainable A process which can be carried out for a long period of time, usually in an environmentally friendly context. For example, in a sustainable forest, trees are planted to replace trees that are chopped down. Page 11

Synthetic An artificial substance or material. Page 22

Tensile strength The ability of material to resist tensile/pulling stresses. Page 70

Tensile testing Testing that measures the response of a material to loading in tension. Page 77

Terms Can be the numbers, single variables or products of variables and/or numbers that make up an equation. Page 37

Testing Sample batches are checked to ensure they are within the customer's specifications for the final product. This determines whether any corrective actions are needed in the manufacturing process. Page 105

Thermal conductivity The ability of material to conduct heat, represented by the letter k. Page 69

Thermoplastic polymers Polymers that can be moulded into different shapes when heated. Page 71

Thermosetting polymers Polymers that do not become mouldable when heated. Page 71

Title block A title block should be displayed on every engineering drawing as it provides vital information about what the drawing contains and also an identification number (under which the drawing is officially filed). Page 29

Tolerance The amount of variation allowed within the dimensions of a product or part being manufactured. Page 33

Torque The force that causes an object to rotate about an axis. It is measured in newton-metres (Nm). Page 64

Total productive maintenance (TPM) A strategy that involves all workers in maintenance activities. Page 136

Toughness The ability of material to absorb impact energy without fracturing. Page 70

Traditional business model A conventional method of structuring and operating a business, usually involving the linear model of production and sales of goods. Page 125

Transfer function Mathematical representation of systems and sub-systems. Page 97

Turbulent flow Flow where fluid particles start to mix in a zig-zag pattern. Page 65

Turnover The rate at which stock is used and replaced. Page 132

Uniformly distributed load A load that is applied evenly over the entire area or length of a beam. Page 80

Unitary PLCs PLCs that have all the different parts and components contained within a single housing. Page 93

Value added Increase in value of a product after each stage of development and production. Page 124

Value stream mapping (VSM) Used to analyse how materials and information flow through a company by 'walking' the process. Page 136

Check your understanding and progress at **www.hoddereducation.co.uk/myrevisionnotes**

Variables Letters used to represent the values in an equation. Page 37

Vector Quantity fully defined by its magnitude, direction and sense. Page 51

Vernier callipers Devices that can be used to measure internal, external or depth measurements using the Vernier scale. Page 62

Viscosity The measurement of a fluid's resistance to flow. Page 65

Visual inspection The use of the naked eye to detect defects. Page 77

Visual management The use of visual tools to communicate information, such as shadow boards and traffic lights. Page 136

(Voltage) potential difference The difference in the electric potential between two points in a circuit, measured in volts (V). Page 85

Welding A joining process which involves heating of a metal and the introduction of a filler rod to form a weld pool that cools and fuses the joint together. Page 74

Wohler test A method of testing fatigue through the use of an S–N curve. Page 77

Young's modulus (E) The ratio of tensile stress (σ) to tensile strain (ε). Page 78

Index

100% sampling inspection 105, 106
  AC (alternating current) 86
  phasor diagrams 87
accidents 113
accountability, organisational 129
accuracy 61
actuators 92, 99
aerodynamics 66
aging (of materials) 76
algebra 37-8
  indices 42
  logarithms 42-3
  progressions 43-4
  quadratic equations 40-1
  simultaneous equations 38-9
alloys 71
amorphous structure 73
analogue signals 88, 96-7
anthropometric data 11
area calculations 45, 49
arithmetic 35-6
arithmetic progression 43-4
artificial intelligence (AI) 22
asphyxiation 119
assets 126-7, 133
  life-cycle management 134
atomic structure 62-3, 72
atoms 62-3, 72
augmented reality (AR) 23
automation 15, 21, 23, 99
averages, measures of 54
beams 80
behaviours
  chemical 63-4
  expected in the workplace 128
Bernoulli's principle 65
BIDMAS, order of calculations 35
binary numbers 55

biomass 18, 19
biometric 24, 25
bonding, solids 72
bottlenecks 134
Boyle's law 67
brazing process, metals 74
British Standards Institute (BSI) 26, 101
budgetary control 134
business models, traditional 125
business practices 125
calculus 45, 46-9
cams 90
capacitance 85
capacitors 87
capacity management 134
Cartesian coordinates 60
casting process, metals 74
ceramics 72
  processing 74
  structures 73
chain dimensioning 33
Charles' law 67
chatbots (or chatterbot) 22
chemical composition 62-3
chemical structure 63
circuit protection systems 87
circular economy 24
circular measurements 49
circular (rotary) motion 64
closed-loop systems 97
cloud computing 24
coating process, metals 74
collaborative working 133-9
combination circuits 86
commercial practices 125
commercial priorities 124
compliance 101

  with legislation 114
composites 71
  history of development 20, 21
  processing 74
  structure 73
compressive strength 70
computer aided manufacture (CAM) 15
concurrent forces 79
conduction 66
conduct, workplace 128
contingency planning 140
continuous improvement 135-7
continuous professional development (CPD) 129
control measures
  in engineering 118
  hierarchy of control 117
  manufacturing quality 16
control systems 17
  applications of 98
  automation 99
  PLCs 93
  theory 96-8
convection 66
coordinates 51, 60
co-planar forces 79
corrosion 76
corrosion resistance 69
costs 124, 126, 132
covalent bonds 72
critical path analysis (CPA) 140
cross (or vector) product 53
crystalline structures 73
cumulative frequency 54
current 84, 86
cyber-physical systems 24
D'Alembert's principle 81

My Revision Notes: Engineering and Manufacturing T Level

dark smoke 121
datum 33
DC (direct current) 86
  circuit networks 87-8
decimal numbers 35, 55
decimal places (d.p.) 36
demand 132
density 69
depreciation 127, 134
design for manufacturing and
    assembly (DFMA) 11
design process 10-12
detail drawings 12, 26
detection 103
diagrams 26
  cause and effect 107
  control systems 98
diagrams see drawings
  phasor 87
  process capability 105
  SOPs 109
differentiation 47-9
digitalisation 23
digital signals 88, 96-7
dimensions 32
  of a triangle 51
  dimensioning 33-4
DMAIC 104
dot (or scalar) product 51, 52
drawings 26
  abbreviations used in 30
  dimensions and tolerances 32-4
  first and third angle 28-9, 32
  information shown in 27-8
  standard features 30-1
  title block 29
  types of 26-7
drones 23
ductility 70
duty holder 111
economic concepts 125-7
eight wastes 135
elasticity 70, 78
elastomers 71
electrical components 92
electrical energy 84
electrical force 84
electrical networks 85
electrical power 84
  key advances 20
electric circuit theories 85-7
electricity 84
  chemicals in 63
  generation of 18-19, 82-3
  health and safety regulations 112
electric motors 20, 82
electrolysis 63
electromagnetic induction 85
electronic components 92
electrons 84
emerging trends in engineering 22-5
energy
  conservation of 80
  distributed 23
  electrical 84

potential and kinetic 81
  sources of 18-19, 82, 120
  stored 116
Engineering Council 101, 102
environmental issues and
    legislation 121-2
equality, diversity and inclusion
    128
equipment
  hazardous 116
  health and safety legislation
    111-12
  maintenance of 120
  measurement 61-2
estimation, statistical 54
ethical codes, workplace 128
European conformity (CE) 101
exponential graphs 46
factorisation method, quadratic
    equations 40-1
factorising 37
failure mode effect analysis (FMEA)
    106
feedback 97
ferrous metals 19, 71
fibre optics 19
financial concepts 126-7
financial responsibility 125-6
fire safety 120
flow characteristics 65
fluid dynamics 65-6
fluid power components 94
fluid power systems 94
fluorescent lighting 20, 22
forces 64-5, 79, 80-3
forging process, metals 74
fossil fuels 82
fractions 36
fracture, material failure 76
friction 81
Gantt charts 140, 141
gauges 62
gears 90
geometric dimensioning and
    tolerancing (GD&T) 33-4
geometric progression 44
geometry 45
global health and safety
    requirements 115
grains in metals 73
graphs 38, 40, 45-7, 50, 78
  SPC control charts 105
gravitational force 81
guarding, machine 120
hardness 70
  testing 77
hazards 111
  health and safety issues 119
  and risk assessment 116-17, 118
health and safety
  environmental laws and issues
    121-2
  legislation 111-14
  responsibilities 115
  risk assessment 116-18

in specific engineering contexts
    118-21
Health and Safety Executive (HSE)
    114, 115
heat 67
heat stress 119
heat transfer 66, 67
heat treatments 75
hexadecimal numbers 55
hierarchical 108
  SOPs 109
hierarchy 125
  of control 117
  organisational 125
histogram 105
history of engineering advances
    20-2
Hooke's law 78
hot working, metals 74
human factors 129-30
hybrid technologies 23
hydraulic systems 94
hydrocarbon gas liquids 18, 19
hydro-electric power 20, 22, 82
hydrostatic pressure 65
hypothesis 60-1
IEE (Institute of Electrical Engineers)
    129
IET (Institution of Engineering and
    Technology) 102, 129
IMechE (Institution of Mechanical
    Engineers) 102, 129
IMI (Institute of the Motor Industry)
    102
imperial (units) 59
incidents 113
indices 42
induction motors 20
inductors 87
infinite series 44
injection moulding 74
injuries 113, 116, 117, 119
innovation in engineering 22-5
input devices 96
inspection 103
  100% sampling 105, 106
  purpose of 104
  stages of 104
  statistical process control (SPC
    105-6
  visual 77
inspectors, health and safety 114
installation 14
integers 35
integration 48
interdependencies, management of
    140
International Organization for
    Standardization (ISO) 101
  ISO 14001, environmental issues
    122
  ISO 9001, quality management
    103
internet of things (IOT) 24
inventory management 132-3

Check your understanding and progress at www.hoddereducation.co.uk/myrevisionnotes

ionic bonds 72
iteration 61
iterative design cycle 11
Izod test (of toughness) 77
just in time (JIT), inventory practice 133
Kaizen 136
Kanban 136
key performance indicators (KPIs) 135
kinetic energy 81
Kirchhoff's current and voltage laws 86
laminar flow 65
latent heat 67
lean manufacturing 136
legislation 101
    environmental 121
    health and safety 111-14
    legal terms used in business 125
levers 91
life cycle
    asset 134
    product 24
    project 138
lifting operations 112
light-emitting diodes (LEDs) 20, 22
linear design process 11
linear equations 38, 45-6, 47
linear motion 64
linkages 91
loads 80
    lifting 91, 112
    load–extension graphs 78
local authorities (LAs) 114, 115
lock out tag out (LOTO) 120
logarithms (logs) 42-3
logic gates 88, 96
made to order 133
made to stock 133
magnetic flux density 85
maintenance 13
    for health and safety 120
    total productive 136
    types of 13
malleability 70
manage by exception 142
manage by stages 142
manual handling operations 111, 112, 120
manufacturing 18
    automation levels 15
    control measures 16
    differing scales of 14
    hazards in 116
    infrastructure/layouts 15
    lean 136
    processes, types of 10
    stock and inventory 132-3
mass production 14, 21
materials
    development of 21
    failure, causes and prevention 76
    heat and surface treatments 75
    mechanical properties 70

physical properties 69
processing techniques 74
testing 77-8
types and structures 71-3
Material Safety Data Sheet (MSDS) 116
mathematics 35-56
matrices 53
matrix working 139
mean 54
measurement
    electrical quantities 85
    equipment 14, 61-2
    principles 61
    statistical 54
    trigonometrical 49-50
    units of 58-9, 84
mechanical work 81
mechanics
    components 90-1
    forces and energy 80-3
    motion, forces and loads 79-80
mechatronics 90-2
    hydraulics and pneumatics 94
    PLCs 93-4
median 54
mental characteristics 130
metallic bonds 72
metallurgical 19
metals 19, 71
    bonding in 72
    chemical reactions of 64
    processing 74
    structure 73
microcontrollers 92
micrometers 62
mode 54
modular PLCs 93
momentum, conservation of 80
motion 64-5
    Newton's three laws of 79
motor driver 93
motors 92
    first electric 20
moulding 74
multimeters 85
multiples 58
necking, materials failure 78
neutrons 62, 63, 72
Newton's laws of motion 79
non-ferrous metals 19, 71
non-value added costs 124
N-type semiconductors 87, 88
nuclear power 19, 82
numbering systems 55
Ohm's law 86
open-loop systems 97
operation effective efficiency (OEE) 136
orthographic drawings 26, 28-9
oscillating motion 64
output devices 96
oxygen use, hazards of 119
parallel circuits 86
parallel dimensioning 33

Pareto analysis 107
PDCA (plan, do, check, act) cycle 135
percentages (%) 36
permit to work (PTW) 119
personal protective equipment (PPE) 111, 112
PERT (project evaluation review technique) charts 140, 141
pharmaceuticals 19
phasor diagrams 86
photovoltaic (PV) 23, 25
physical characteristics 130
planning techniques, projects 140-1
PLCs (programmable logic controllers) 93
pneumatic 19
pneumatic systems 94
point load 80
polar coordinates 60
polymers 71
    crosslinking of 73
    processing 74
potential difference (voltage) 85
potential divider circuits 86
potential energy 81
power 81
    electrical 20, 84
    fluid 94
power generation 18-19, 23, 82
power series 44
power sources 24, 82-3
pressure 64, 65, 67
preventative maintenance 13
probabilities 54
process capability 105
process devices 96
product life cycle 24
professional conduct and responsibilities 130-1
professional engineering bodies 101-2, 129
professional recognition 129
professional standards 129
programmable logic controllers (PLCs) 93
project brief 138
project control 141-2
project evaluation review technique (PERT) chart 140, 141
(project) life cycle 138
project management 138-9
project managers 139
project planning and control 140-2
protons 62, 63, 72, 84
P-type semiconductors 87-8
pulleys 91
Pythagoras' theorem 49
quadratic equations 40-1
    single point of inflexion 48
qualitative data 12
quality assurance (QA) 16, 102-4
quality circles 107
quality control (QC) 16, 102-3
quality improvement 106-8
quality management 101-8

quality standards 101, 103
quantitative data 12
radians (rad) 49-50
radiation 66
range 54
ratios 36
reactive maintenance 13
reciprocating motion 64
recyclability of a material 69
recycling 24, 69, 121, 122
redundant stock 132
regulations see legislation
renewable energy/power sources 18, 24, 82
research 12
resistance 84
resistors 87
resources 124
    needed for project plans 140
risk assessment 112, 116-18
risk management 138
robotics 15, 23
roles and responsibilities
    in projects 139-40
    in the workplace 128-9
rolling (of metals) 74
rotary motion 64, 92
sacrificial anode 76
sampling 104, 105-6
SCADA (Supervisory Control and Data Acquisition) 93
scalar quantities 53, 59
    dot (or scalar) product 51, 52
scale 36
scales of manufacturing 14
schematics 26-7, 98
science
    chemical composition and behaviours 62-4
    fluid dynamics 65-6
    forces and motion 64-5
    measurement 61-2
    scientific methods 60-1
    thermodynamics 66-7
    units of measurement 58-9
    vector and coordinate measuring systems 59-60
scientific method 60-1
sectors of engineering industry 17-19
semiconductors 87-8
sensible heat 67
sensors 92, 99
sensory stimuli 23, 25
series circuits 86
signals 88, 96-7

significant figures (s.f.) 36
SI (metric) units 58
    conversion to imperial 59
    electrical parameters 84
simplifying equations 37
simply supported beams 80
simultaneous equations 38, 39
single minute exchange of dies (SMED) 136
sintering process, metals 74
six S (6S) steps 136
Six Sigma 104, 106
smart materials 72
solar power 23, 82, 83
solutions (mixtures) 63
specification 10, 16
specification limits 104, 105
spontaneous combustion 119
stakeholders 139
standard deviation 54
standard form 35
standardised incidence ratio (SIR) 113
Standard Operating Procedures (SOPs) 108-9
standards, professional 26, 101, 103, 129
statistical analysis 54
statistical process control (SPC) 105-6
stock and inventory principles and practices 132-3
stored (potential) energy 81, 116, 118
straight-line graphs 46, 47
strain (in materials) 78
stress
    from hot environments 119
    in materials 70, 78
structure
    atomic 62-3, 72
    chemical 63
    of materials 72-3
subject of an equation 37-8
submultiples 58
summing points 97-8
surface treatments 75
sustainability 24
sustainable design 11
sustainable power sources 82
synthetic 22
technological advances 20-2
television (TV) 21
tensile strength 70
tensile testing 77
terms (in an equation) 37
testing 12, 105

of materials 77
    and quality assurance 103
thermal conductivity (k) 69
thermodynamics 66-8
thermoplastic polymers 71
thermosetting polymers 71, 74
thrust 65, 66
timber 72
title block 29
tolerance 33, 61
    tolerancing 33-4
tools 14
torque 64, 65
total productive maintenance (TPM) 136
total quality management (TQM) 103
toughness (of a material) 70
    testing of 77
traceability 103
traditional business models 125
transfer functions 97
trigonometry 49-51
    graphs 46
turbulent flow 65
turnover 132
uniformly distributed load 80
unitary PLCs 93
units of measurement 58-9, 84
value added 124
value stream mapping (VSM) 136, 137
variables 37
vector quantities 59
vectors 51-3
Vernier callipers 62
virtual reality (VR) 23
viscosity 65
visual inspection 77
visual management 136
(voltage) potential difference 85-6
volume calculations 45
waste disposal 19, 24
    methods of 122
    regulations 121
wastes within a business 135
    reducing 136
waves 88
welding 74
wind power 82, 83
Wohler test 77
workplace
    health and safety 111-22
    responsibilities 128-9
'write downs', inventory 132
Young's modulus (E) 78

Check your understanding and progress at **www.hoddereducation.co.uk/myrevisionnotes**